PRAISE FOR PRA

God gives people trumpets. Some are scared to touch them. Others put them in a closet and shut the door. Donica Hudson is a woman who picked up her trumpet and is sounding the alarm for our nation. *Pray America Great* reveals her faith, courage and godly insight. Be encouraged. But more importantly, heed this dynamic call to action.

~Robert Whitlow, Esq.
Best-selling Author of *Chosen People*

Donica Hudson is a voice of clarity making sense out of the senseless and shedding light on what is happening in America today. With clarity comes understanding, and with understanding comes peace. *Pray America Great* will bring peace in tumultuous times.

~Dr. Lance Wallnau
International Speaker, Best-selling Author, Trainer
LanceWallnau.com

Donica Hudson has a victory message for our day. In *Pray America Great*, she has shown light on the darkness in our country and lifted up the true answer of covenant with God as our strength. Culture ultimately carries in its wake the politics of a nation. Therefore, the victory message Donica has written to each of us: appeal to heaven, bend the knee to God, fight forward clad in the armor of God, and repair the breach by the power of His Holy Spirit, not only transforms individual lives but also builds a culture that sparks a nationwide Jesus awakening.

~Tom Phillips
Vice President, Billy Graham Evangelistic Association, Author

"I'm doing a great work; I can't come down." Nehemiah's words in Chapter 6, V. 2 must have been ringing in Donica's ears as she poured out her heart and soul in this outstanding prayer book. This engaging book informs and equips readers for the battle to preserve our nation and our Judeo-Christian culture for ourselves and our progeny.

~Dr. Carol M. Swain, retired Vanderbilt Professor, Host of *Be the People Podcast*

If there is a prayer warrior who gets what is at stake, it is Donica Hudson. Her book *Pray America Great* is a rich source of information for those who are called by His name to pray.

~Nancy Schulze
Founder, Republican Congressional Wives Speakers
National Women for Trump Advisory Board
Strategic Consultant and Board Member, Physicians for Reform

You hold in your hands a tool that attests to an aspect of the essential nature of your life and the possibility that future generations depend on what you do with it. Human beings are made for eternity, two parts spirit and soul and one part body of flesh. Actual events in the U.S. at this writing could not more strongly attest to the mandate of *Pray America Great* to come into agreement with heaven and wrestle the future of generations out of the creeping grip of darkness. We are participators in God's activity to reclaim His inheritance of nations. *Pray America Great: Joining the Prayer Force of Heaven* is an accounting of natural and spiritual events coinciding and colliding that have tremendous relevance for every person. In it, Donica Hudson sets forth a handbook of discovery for Christians to take their place as the sons and daughters of God for whom "all creation groans in travail looking for their appearing." Whether you live in the U.S. or another nation, you will be glad should you decide to join heaven's prayer force and become a part of making everlasting history.

~Bonnie Chavda, All Nations Church
The Watch of the Lord Prayer Movement

We are living in a time in history when our Father is releasing a clarion call for the warriors and gatekeepers of our nation to command their post to protect the sovereignty of our land. Donica has answered the call through this God-inspired work, *Pray America Great*. May the truth revealed on the pages of this book reverberate throughout every home and bring healing to the soul of this great country.

~Linda Vega
CEO Firot Capital Solutions LLC
Founder, Awakened in Prayer Ministries International

PRAY AMERICA GREAT

Joining the Prayer Force of Heaven

Dearest Jackee
You are a treasure! Thank you for connecting me with some wonderful kingdom believers. Together, we will

DONICA HUDSON

pray third heaven prayers to Save America! *Love You Dearly!*

BOSS

M E D I A *Donica*

Isaiah 58:12

Distributed globally by Boss Media.
New York | Los Angeles | London | Sydney

Hardcover ISBN: 978-1-63337-431-7
Paperback ISBN: 978-1-63337-430-0
E-book ISBN: 978-1-63337-432-4
LCCN: 2020917570

Manufactured and printed in the United States of America

This book is lovingly dedicated to the memory of my late father, Donald C. Perry, who served as Judge Advocate General in the U.S. Airforce during the Vietnam War and provided the inspiration for developing a "United Prayer Force" to Pray America Great.

The late Donald C. Perry and daughter Donica Perry Hudson

CONTENTS

ACKNOWLEDGMENTS

TO MY AMAZING FAMILY, thank you for supporting me with love, prayers, time away to write, meals brought to my desk, and encouragement. There's no way I would have ever gotten this done without your faithful support and understanding.

So much has happened since I began writing this book in January 2019. The most difficult thing was losing Mom as we all cared for her in our home. There were times when I thought I was never going to have the desire to finish the book because of the demands of being a caretaker and the grief of watching Mom suffer for so long. But we all rallied together, and God saw us through. I can't help but think that Mom's cheering us on from the cloud of witnesses in heaven.

My husband Todd, thank you for combing over the manuscript and offering great advice. Thank you for willingly sharing your "windfall" surprise with me to help publish this book. You are the best and have always been my rock.

My son Davis, I would be remiss if I did not thank you for your support and civic encouragement. The silver lining of the COVID-19 "plandemic" was having you home from the mission field. I guess it's befitting that you won "Most Likely to Be the Next Donald Trump" at YWAM. You truly understand and embody dual citizenship, dual commissions, and dual commandments. Plus, you can hold your own in any debate—true "Charlie Kirk style!"

My daughter Salem, thank you for your help in getting the guest quarters ready for my publisher when she came. I'm going to miss you while you're on the mission field! I'm thankful that you see clearly the state of our country and speak out about it.

My son Lucas, thank you for bringing me food or meals followed by "Mama hugs." You and your siblings make life on Earth worth fighting for.

Sheila Cogan, thank you for helping me for forty-five hours straight one weekend with research and manuscript completion. And that's just the tip of the iceberg! I just love how the Holy Spirit tells you exactly where to go to find old archival video scripts and book references. Thank you for your expertise in video production and website building. You are so gifted. Don't know what I'd do without you!

Mike and Debra Kerr, you believed in me and in this call to write this book from day one. Thank you for sowing into this work with finances, prayer, and prophecy. Mike, you should be happy to see your prophetic word about a flag fulfilled in this book for God's Kingdom purposes.

Pastor Tony and Lee Mazzone, thank you for supporting me in so many astounding ways. Moving nearby to help pioneer this ministry hub and sowing into the publishing of this book have left me speechless. Thank you, Lee, for helping go over manuscript portions and bringing food for my publisher when she came and stayed with us.

Larry and Maggie, thank you for your support and prayers. Larry, thank you for sharing your wonderful design expertise in creating the Prayer Force logo. I'm so thankful you guys moved here from California. Thank you, Maggie, for bringing the *Constitution Alive!* study series to our church group.

Dom and Heather, thank you for your support. Heather, I'm so thankful to God for bringing you to me as a bookkeeper and prayer partner. May He open the doors for much more ministry!

Joy Lamb, thank you for that amazing interview before the 2016 election. I had no idea at the time that it would be a pivotal moment in my life that is recorded in this book. Thank you for your prayers and support for this book.

Jim Quick, my broadcast partner, thank you for your help with creating the donation website, producing videos, and creating dynamic broadcasts like the March for Life and the Trump Rally. I look forward to all that we will accomplish in the future for the Kingdom.

Pastors Ken and Priscilla Davis, thank you for your prayer support and encouragement through your own book publishing experiences. So thankful you are with us in ministry. Priscilla, thank you for helping take care of our media guests during the writing of this book. Ken, thanks for facilitating our constitutional study on Fridays. America needs you!

Much thanks to Craig Seibert for collaborating through the years in prayer and the historical context of recovenanting. Your teachings in www.ChristianCitizenshipTraining.org are a blessing to all.

Jane Miller, thank you for the yummy meals for my publisher and her husband. You have such a gift of hospitality.

Robin Johnson, thank you for believing in me and supporting the book. Thanks for sharing your wonderful food with my publisher as well. You and Alex are a blessing to our family.

Robert Whitlow, thanks for throwing that Appeal to Heaven flag over my shoulders and encouraging me with your prophetic wisdom. This book is one of the fruits of that act of obedience. Thank you and Kathy for your love, prayers, and support.

Pastor Andre, most of this crazy faith activist prayer journey is because of you! I thought I was just doing a TV show interview in 2006 with you, but it turned into a video series on Native American Reconciliation ending with a foot-washing ceremony in Murphy, North Carolina. Then in 2013, I thought I was just doing a radio interview with you which turned into a mandate to write a Prayer Proclamation for North Carolina's governor to sign and then a call to mail that signed proclamation to all fifty U.S. governors! I better not do anymore interviews with you for a while unless I want another three- to ten-year assignment! Lol!

Ruben, thank you for always calling to encourage me at exactly the right times when Mom was passing, when I was grieving, when I was writing, and when God was speaking! Your supernatural words in due season have helped to sustain me and to guide a lot of the writing in this book.

Winstona, Elaine, Tonya, Ouida and Debbie, Lisa, Lori, Charlotte, Pam, Christie, Adrienne and Mel, thank you for covering me in prayer as I suffered the loss of my mom in the middle of this writing and as I labored over deadlines and securing funds for the book. You are amazing prayer warriors.

ACKNOWLEDGMENTS

Suzanne and Bonnie, thank you for your generous input and your support of this book. We are a three-stranded cord of prayer that will not be broken!

Michelle, I am so grateful that God led me to you for publishing. Your team, especially Sherrie and Emily, is incredible. So thankful for you all.

Karen Noble, thank you for your continued friendship and partnership in prayer over this book and over life that has sustained me through the years. Love you.

Last but not least, to the one who empowered me to overcome by His own blood, I give thanks.

FOREWORD

THE FIRST TIME I INVITED Donica Hudson to lead prayer on my national prayer line, she and I bonded. Donica's prayers took me into the third heaven, which very few people have ever done. She is a voice of clarity and force in prayer for such a time as this. God is using her like a modern-day Esther to stand in the gap for our nation.

When Donica gave me the *Pray America Great* manuscript, the Lord told me to clear my schedule and go into my prayer room because this manuscript is His first priority. You are holding in your hands a classic prayer book.

Pray America Great: Joining the Prayer Force of Heaven was taken out of the very vaults from the courtroom of heaven, where the Lord downloaded and placed the very essence of Himself into the manuscript Donica has produced. It was not just a good idea but a God idea that was part of His original plan for creation. God Himself would be the foundation and the chief cornerstone of this nation.

When God spoke "pray America great" into the atmosphere, no longer was it a logos word, but it became His breath and His sound, living rhema words that took root and began joining the states, once again to be united as His original masterpiece, once again to become the covenant United States of America.

The first original sin was not the act of disobedience of eating the fruit of the tree of knowledge of good and evil; evil was when Lucifer challenged the divine authority and order of worship that only belongs to the Lord Jesus Christ. Obviously, the second sin was when Adam disobeyed God's simple instructions not to eat of the tree of knowledge of good and evil. These instructions were given to Adam even *before* Eve was formed from him. Adam had the responsibility and duty to set boundaries and divine order in place, which he did not do. He stood with Eve and did not stop her from eating the forbidden fruit. Instead, he joined her. It is interesting that those two original sins—challenging divine authority and failing to obey the Lord's boundaries, including much manipulation (witchcraft)—continue to be the root cause of the chaos that is trying to plague our nation even now.

Our forefathers came to this land seeking a life of religious liberty and freedom. With much prayer and fasting, seeking the face of their Lord and Master Jesus Christ, they set the same boundaries that were written into the Torah and the Bible long ago. Being fully aware of His sovereignty, they made sure all their worship went to Him and to Him alone. They also understood honor and respect, which is a commandment from the God of Abraham, Isaac, and Jacob, promising long life. This promise extends to the people of the United States who choose with their votes to represent God in this great land and nation.

During Rosh Hashanah of September 1992, while pastoring Orlando Christian Center, I was jolted out of my sleep and quickly went to our family room, which was my sanctuary (secret place) where I spent many all-nighters in prayer. This night was different. It was the only time where I heard the audible voice of the Lord that was somewhat frightening with the fear of the Lord. His voice thundered and said,

> *I will shake everything that can be shaken. Only those people who have their feet on the ground, eyes on Me—people of character and integrity—will be able to stand through this. I will allow you to see things and hear things. You do what I tell you to do, say what I tell you to say. When obedience is done, disobedience will be punished!*
>
> *This is an assignment that only you can do. When it happens, it will happen in the fall of the year and something will happen around Thanksgiving time.*

This is that time!

Judgement always begins in the house of the Lord and then goes to the world. **We still have a small window of time to reexamine ourselves first and repent of any known or unknown sins and quickly come back to the foot of the cross at His altar.**

Donica, like her father who was a constitutionalist and a lawyer, knows she has a God-given assignment that only she can fulfill with the torch of her father that He has placed in her hand. She carries on the mandate and presses toward the mark of the high calling.

She is tenacious, obedient, and resilient. She is able to withstand and recover quickly from difficult conditions. Donica knows she was chosen to be a prophetic trailblazer, blazing trails beyond anything that history has ever seen before.

Be prepared to be totally undone as you read this book like I was when the Lord told me to take this manuscript into my prayer room and shut the door. Like a Holy Ghost missile, we must be prepared individually and corporately to return to our first love, to prayer, and to the cross. We must obey the Word which says, *"If my people, which are called by My name, shall humble themselves, and pray, and seek My face, and turn from their wicked ways: then will I hear from heaven, and will forgive their sin, and will heal their land" (2 Chronicles 7:14).*

In the early 90s, the Lord gave my mom, Pauline Harthern, five words:

1. Intercession
2. Repentance
3. Revival
4. Harvest
5. Second coming

I believe we are prophetically and historically between number one (Intercession) and number two (Repentance), which must happen before true revival—greater than history has ever seen—before the greatest harvest of souls on Earth takes place. Then we will see Him face to face.

BUCKLE UP!

—Suzanne Hinn, Minister and Intercessor
Founder, Suzanne Hinn National Prayer Call
Founder, Purifying Fire International Ministries

INTRODUCTION

SHOCK. DISBELIEF. PANIC. ANGER... then outrage. These are the emotions that flooded me when my fourteen-year-old daughter Salem ran up to me with a fear-stricken face at our local grocery store.

"Mom, there was a man in the women's restroom with me!"

"What? Are you okay? What was he doing?" I asked, heart racing with alarm.

"I'm okay . . . kinda freaked out. He was washing his hands in the sink."

"Do you think he accidentally went into the wrong bathroom?" I was desperately trying to find some logic, some legitimate reason why a man would be in the women's bathroom.

"No. When I came out of the stall, he kept on washing his hands like he had a right to be there. It was creepy," Salem said.

Getting angrier by the minute, I asked, "What was the guy wearing?"

"Black pants and black T-shirt," she responded.

I ran into the women's restroom; he was gone. I quizzed Salem for more details and looked around the store for a guy who matched the description—all black attire; short, brown hair; about six feet tall—but I couldn't find him.

The mama bear in me was furious. A man dressed as a man, using one of the stalls in a women's public restroom and washing his hands unashamedly alongside my teenage daughter and other ladies was *totally unacceptable*! Did he peek between the stall doors at the women . . . at my daughter? What would he have done to my daughter if there had *not* been other women in the restroom at the time? My daughter should have a right to privacy, dignity, and safety!

I knew the culprit—the bathroom bill soon to take effect in Charlotte—was bleeding out to my Matthews suburb. Men were already beginning to use women's restrooms, even if they weren't within Charlotte city limits!

I recalled a conversation I had overheard weeks previously at a restaurant in the North Carolina Mountains. Sitting at a table next to ours was about fourteen guys and girls from a wedding party. One of the guys asked the others, "Hey, have you heard about the new bathroom bill in Charlotte?"

Another guy responded, "I don't know much about it."

The first guy then elaborated, "Yeah, you can use whatever bathroom you want."

No one at the table contested this misguided claim. *Could you imagine how dangerous our bathrooms would be if this were the "group think"?*

Standing there in the grocery store with my teenage daughter, I didn't have to think anymore this bathroom bill was dangerous!

Enraged as I was, I felt powerless—like my children were being fed to the lions.

This bathroom bill was already approved by the Charlotte City Council and set to go into effect.

Is this *really* how we were going to be forced to live in America, in the North Carolina *I* grew up in, where moms and dads are filled with fear when their kids go to school and are forced to share bathrooms, locker rooms, and even showers with members of the opposite biological sex?

I'd read the ludicrous bathroom bill. I knew all it took for a man to legally access those areas designated to women only was for him to claim he "felt like a woman" that day. How many perverts, deluded voyeurs, and pedophiles were going to fake femininity to satisfy their lusts? Would my daughter become a victim? Would my sons even be safe?

I knew from my TV broadcast experience in Charlotte that sexual immorality was a serious stronghold in the "Queen City." I'd hosted a local TV show called *Charlotte Alive* and reported on revival and spiritual awakening in the Charlotte Metrolina area. Before each quarter's TV tapings, my team and I would pray over which "mountain of culture" (government, church, media, family, arts and entertainment, education, and business) to focus on and the related strongholds blocking revival. When our team tackled the stronghold of sexual immorality, we encountered the worst warfare of any quarterly TV tapings in five years—always a clear sign to believers of the principality at work over a city (Ephesians 6:12).

So I knew this bathroom encounter was a spiritual battle that required another level of prayer—radical prayer.

"BEEN HERE" BEFORE

I had been leading citywide prayer events since the attack on America on September 11, 2001, when the world watched in horror as terrorists crashed planes into the Twin Towers in New York City and into our nation's Pentagon—killing thousands. On the countdown to that first anniversary, my ministry team and I hosted Uplift Charlotte, which was thirty-five days of 24-7 prayer. It culminated into a citywide prayer vigil called Uplift America on September 11, 2002, centered in downtown Charlotte and covered by the local Fox News.

Charlotte Mayor and future Governor Pat McCrory came; North Carolina legislative representatives came, and authorities from all seven mountains of culture came, and they agreed with us in prayer to save America. I taped a video invitation to President Bush, and he sent a video response, which I played at the prayer event.

Our theme was 2 Chronicles 7:14: *"If My people, who are called by My name, will humbles themselves and pray and seek My face and turn from their wicked ways, then will I hear from heaven, and I will forgive their sin and heal their land."*

In April 2004, we hosted Metrolina Prayer Vigil where pastors, youth, and worshippers ministered in tents for three days around the clock. Our focal point was Acts 15:16–18: *"After this I will return and rebuild David's fallen tent. Its ruins I will rebuild, and I will restore it, that the rest of mankind may seek the Lord, even all the Gentiles who bear my name, says the Lord, who does these things— things known from long ago.*

Later in 2004, we rented a movie theatre and hosted prayer before the showing of *The Passion of the Christ* produced by Mel Gibson. I've led prayer at the North Carolina Legislative Chapel, privately praying with senators, congressional representatives, and other prominent government leaders. I've had the honor of leading prayer and devotions at the Billy Graham Evangelistic Association. I've led prayer on national prayer calls, on TV and radio, on webcasts, and on Zoom calls.

Can you tell I believe in prayer?

However, when my daughter encountered the man in a women's restroom because of a ridiculous bathroom bill, I knew it was time to not only be a hearer of the Word but also to be a doer! Sometimes, we need to put feet to our faith.

KICKED INTO ACTION

With decades of prayer under my belt, I would *not* remain silent while my children suffered the consequences of rogue government prejudice toward minority special-interest groups—transgenders, who make up .03 percent of the population. They already had private bathroom and facility accommodations under Title IX of our Constitution. The "PC" (political correctness) crowd had gone too far! I don't expect everyone, including transgenders, to believe like I do, but I do expect laws in our land to keep *everyone* safe.

My husband and I took action! We worked with Alliance Defending Freedom and sued the federal government for not protecting our children in bathrooms, locker rooms, and showers.

Speaking at NC Capital on HB2

We helped form an activist group called North Carolinians for Privacy. I was interviewed on the radio and TV and by newspaper reporters. I spoke on a platform at the steps of the North Carolina General Assembly in Raleigh to a large crowd of citizens and media, spoke in the pouring rain at the Charlotte City Government Plaza multiple times, at multiple press conferences, and before the Charlotte City Council, did an interview in my home for the Daily Signal (Heritage Foundation), posted on social media, contacted the governor, signed petitions, worked with local conservative agencies—you name it, I used every form of media and government activism I could to protect my children—and myself for that matter!

If your city has such a bathroom bill, then lazy, innocent, and carefree days of American baseball, hot dogs, and apple pie can

IF YOUR CITY HAS SUCH A BATHROOM BILL, THEN LAZY, INNOCENT, AND CAREFREE DAYS OF AMERICAN BASEBALL, HOT DOGS, AND APPLE PIE CAN NO LONGER BE ENJOYED WHEN YOUR CHILDREN CAN BE EASILY MOLESTED IN THE STADIUM BATHROOM.

no longer be enjoyed when your children can be easily molested in the stadium bathroom.

Does anyone hear me?

SEASON OF WAR

When my husband and I brought a lawsuit against the federal government in 2016, I knew we were entering a season of war as believers. And we are still in that season of war . . . *only now, we aren't merely fighting a bathroom bill; we're fighting to preserve our nation's U.S. Constitution!* All across America, we're fighting for the right to live out our deeply held religious convictions without government interference. We're battling a powerful "fake-news" media that's teamed up with extreme liberal ideology and deep-state conspirators who illegally spied on the Trump campaign, accused an innocent sitting president of Russian collusion, and then falsely tried to impeach him! We are in a battle to save America spiritually, constitutionally, and economically.

My friend Lance Wallnau explained on a live webinar that there are 170 nations that cannot participate in the global banking game. If the value of the American dollar falls as the global standard, so goes democracy, tumbling the 170 nations into the "valley of decision" in a domino effect toward Marxism and totalitarianism. Consequently, China will be effectively secured as the world leader,[1] which will move us toward a one-world government. China is barbarically torturing and sexually abusing Muslims in concentration camps.[2] Trump was spot-on to focus on China during his 2016 candidacy. And the deep state knew it.

The first horrendous lie to be peddled to the American people was that President Donald Trump and his campaign colluded with Russia to win the 2016 presidential election.

It's little wonder why 77 percent of Americans across the political spectrum disapprove of Congress's job performance, according to the latest survey from Gallup.

For more than two years, Congressional Democrats excused inaction by attacking President Donald J. Trump every day for a crime he did not commit. The Mueller Report—a 400-page document that cost American taxpayers at least $35 million—recommended no charges against the president. That should have ended the matter.

Instead, Democrats have a new obstruction strategy: weaponize the subpoena powers of Congress to fish for political ammunition to use against the Trump administration.

The mainstream media always plays along, and it denies any accomplishments or progress that could risk making an opponent look good. The price tag—broken trust—comes later.

- Today, 4 percent of Americans say they have a great deal of trust in Congress.
- In 2016, Americans' confidence in mass media hit its lowest level in history.
- Between 1958 and 2015, public trust in Washington plunged from 73 percent to 18 percent.[3]

Socialism has so infiltrated America's educational system and left-leaning political leaders that:

- 60 percent of millennials "strongly support" government-funded college tuition *paid for by you.*

- 69 percent of millennials support "Medicare for all"— *paid for by you.*
- 50 percent of millennials said they "would prefer to live in a socialist country."[4]

Most of these millennials have no idea that voting for the AOCs (Democratic Representative Alexandria Ocasio-Cortez) and Democratic Senator Bernie Sanders of the country and their socialist values will condemn us to a Venezuelan death. Current political correctness is priming America to gulp down the toxic cocktail of Sharia law mixed with socialism and a twist of Marxism where government is God, and Jews and Christians are persecuted and jailed.

Liberals unable to digest the fact that Trump won fair and square are now trying to destroy our brilliant U.S. Constitutional Electoral College system so that the L.A. and New York liberal populous can determine the future of all fifty states. Our Founding Fathers had the wise foresight to set up an Electoral College process that decentralizes our elections, so our entire country has the most amount of representation possible. This prevents tyranny by popular vote and minimizes election fraud.

If you think millennials are deceived, look at the stats on their successors, Gen Z (Generation Z):

The Barna Group just released a new study of Generation Z (current teenagers) that found they are the least-Christian generation in US history. Nearly twice as many claims to be atheists as Millineals (13% to 7%), and 35% of current teens say that they are either atheist, agnostic or unaffiliated with any religion. Just 59% say they are Catholic or Christian (a six-point drop from the Millennial generation), and only 4% hold what is considered a true Biblical worldview.

The survey places the cause of this change on today's teenagers having been brought up in a post-Christian, post-modern environment where they've never been exposed to Christianity or church. I [author Mike Huckabee] would have guessed from looking at the results that their parents allowed pop culture to replace traditional Christian values as the #1 influence in their kids' lives, and it's showing up in other harmful ways as well.[5]

Gen Z parents are not the only ones allowing pop culture to replace traditional Christian values. The Church is also falling into the trap of allowing social justice to replace biblical righteousness. With social justice, moral relativism prevails, and culture makes up its own rules, meaning that there are no biblical absolutes.

> THE CHURCH IS ALSO FALLING INTO THE TRAP OF ALLOWING SOCIAL JUSTICE TO REPLACE BIBLICAL RIGHTEOUSNESS.

Biblical righteousness, or right standing with God, is imputed through entering into a covenant with God through Jesus's sinless shed blood. It's called the "covenant of grace"—one that most of the Founding Fathers who crafted our Constitution had entered into when they accepted Jesus as Lord and Savior.

In looking at today's America, we can see how far we have fallen from the faith of our Founding Fathers who risked their lives to secure freedom. In our country right now, *we the people* are learning that former administrations elected to *uphold* the law may be guilty of treason and criminal offenses as the evil abyss of the deep state is continually being exposed.

THE DEEP STATE AND PEDOPHILE ISLAND

Even uglier than potential treason, the American public has looked on with *horror* as the Trump administration has boldly exposed and begun prosecuting a global pedophiliac ring, beginning with the late Jeffrey Epstein. Epstein was the owner of "Pedophile Island," and he mysteriously died in prison before his trial. And it looks like a lot of global leaders, Hollywood celebrities. and influential U.S. politicians are involved in this outrageous sickening sexual abuse of children.

Meanwhile, *we the people* are so snowed that we are electing "puppet" congressional representatives like socialist AOC, a former bartender who *auditioned as an actress on video* for her spot to run for Congress.[6] Unbelievable! No wonder her team controls her socialist messaging. Additionally, our cities are being bombarded by Soros-funded activist groups operating by Saul Alinsky's book, *Rules For Radicals*, aimed at destroying our nation's democratic form of government from the inside out.[7]

We the people are losing America!

In the process of fighting for my constitutional rights to protect my children and to preserve my freedom of religion, I learned that the most effective weapon for battle is *PRAYER!* Without prayer, the bathroom bill in North Carolina would not have been defeated. Without prayer, there is no victory! Without prayer, the forces of heaven are not summoned! Without prayer, Founding Father George Washington would not have won the Revolutionary War for America.

In the freezing winter of 1777, General George Washington was burdened with the lack of supplies for his troops camped at Valley Forge and with the overwhelming superiority of the British forces. Soldiers died at the rate of twelve per day, with many not even having blankets or shoes.[8]

A Quaker named Potts came upon Washington "interceding for his beloved country."[9] That night, Potts told his wife, "I have seen this day what I shall never forget. Till now I have thought that a Christian and a soldier were characters incompatible; but if George Washington be not a man of God, I am mistaken, and still more shall I be disappointed if God does not through him perform some great thing for this country."[10]

Throughout the war, as it was understood in his military family, George Washington gave a part of every day to private prayer and devotion.[11]

> *When ye pray, say, Our Father which art in heaven,*
> *Hallowed be thy name. Thy kingdom come. Thy will be done,*
> *as in heaven, so in earth.*
> *~The Lord's Prayer*

Without prayer, Abraham Lincoln would not have been able to abolish slavery when the North won the Civil War.[12] We need that kind of prayer in America now.

Radical changes to culture require radical prayer, the kind of prayer of the ages that summons the forces of heaven and preserves the foundations of America!

Won't you join me as we unite with the forces of covenant and history to

RADICAL CHANGES TO CULTURE REQUIRE RADICAL PRAYER.

PRAY AMERICA GREAT?

CHAPTER 1
WARNED

IT WAS JUNE 2015. A female had been washed up on the beach, face down. Her arm was several feet away—oh no! And there was another detached limb lying in the surf on the other side of her.

I was bewildered. What had happened?

Golden blond loose curls tangled with seaweed were rising and falling with the ebb and flow of the surf. She was surrounded by dirty sea-foam.

> THIS WAS A CRIME SCENE, AND I WAS THE ONLY ONE THERE.

This was a crime scene, and I was the only one there. I peered over the female's broken body to see if I recognized her.

It was Lady Liberty!

As I woke up from the dream in that beachfront hotel, deep sadness tinged with fear washed over me.

Immediately, I knew America was in serious trouble—liberty and justice were at stake.

Hours later, I knew the reason for my grave dream. Just down the street from us, a deranged white supremacist massacred nine black Christians during a prayer service at Emanuel African Methodist Episcopal Church, one of Charleston's oldest churches and sites for organizing civil rights.

My girlfriends and I were devastated at the news. This was no longer carefree beach vacation time. This was wartime—war on our knees. These were our brothers and sisters in Christ who had been attacked and murdered minutes away from us.

How could America have returned to so much racial hatred?

The dream was God's way of clueing me into what was happening to America's foundations. For the Statue of Liberty to be toppled and dismembered in my dream was a clear sign of the devastation to come.

Can we stop the destruction?

The answer to that question keeps me on my knees.

I knew in the dream that the dismembering of Lady Liberty in the surf represented babies being dismembered in the womb (now even *outside* the womb) and ensuing judgment against America if we do not repent and overturn Roe v. Wade, which was a great offense to God. I also knew that America's sin of racism and slavery was going to be the weapon the devil used to try to destroy her.

My jaw dropped when I studied my friend, Craig Seibert's, Christian Civics Training Initiative's message on the true meaning of the Statue of Liberty. The idea for Lady Liberty originated at a dinner party in France in 1865, just after the end of the U.S. Civil War! So she was conceived after America's battle that ended slavery in America. And here I'd had a dream of her destruction the morning of the Charleston massacre.

What had happened to America? Why were we regressing?

This massacre marked the beginning of the many times the Lord would speak to me about the tragic state of our nation and commission me to take action, both on my knees in prayer and in the public square. Our country could not go on like this, and I had to do something about it.

I write these experiences and offer guidelines for prayer in hopes that this book will help others who face the same battles in the future (Matthew 13:52 ESV). I pray that our children will learn two lessons from it—the strategies of the enemy and the supernatural intelligence that God provides us from heaven to help us come out victorious.

> MAY ALL WHO HAVE LOST HOPE REMEMBER THAT JESUS HAS ALREADY WON THE BATTLE.

May our future generations keep the victories for which we have fought that secured their liberties. May the legacy of our Christian heritage stand and save America.

And may all who have lost hope remember that Jesus has already won the battle.

And now, go, write it before them on a tablet and inscribe it in a book, that it may be for the time to come as a witness forever (Isaiah 30:8 ESV).

CHAPTER 2

DESTRUCTION OF AMERICA

DID ANYONE EVER BELIEVE in a million years that we would be forbidden by government in many states to sing in church?

Yes, I know there are valid health reasons for not spreading COVID-19, but it's alarming to see church gatherings banned and yet watch massive gatherings in the thousands of citywide protests that are perfectly legal and deemed "essential."

Dr. Jeff Barkey said it well while speaking at a California rally that was recorded. The video went viral,

DID ANYONE EVER BELIEVE IN A MILLION YEARS THAT WE WOULD BE FORBIDDEN BY GOVERNMENT IN MANY STATES TO SING IN CHURCH?

What if quarantining the healthy doesn't actually save lives? What if wearing a mask in public is not effective? Never in the history of this great republic have we quarantined the healthy.

29

Never in the history of this great republic have we told church-goers that it's illegal for you to exercise your First Amendment right of freedom of religion. Yet at the same time, it's essential to keep pot dispensaries open. Never in the history of this country have we been told that you can't go to church because it's nonessential, but you can go and get an abortion because that's essential. Never before in our country have we let criminals out of jail, but we've told you, you can't exercise your Second Amendment right and protect yourself by purchasing a firearm. When liquor stores are deemed essential, but your businesses are deemed nonessential, there's something wrong going on.[1]

Then Dr. Barkey pulled out a pocket booklet, held it up, and declared, "This booklet, our Declaration of Independence and U.S. Constitution, was never designed to restrain the people. It was designed to restrain the government!"[2]

Near the end of his poignantly well-delivered speech, Dr. Barkey stated, "As a physician, I can tell you, yes, this virus is dangerous. But as we see the statistics come in, we're realizing that the fatality rate of this virus is in the ballpark of a bad seasonal influenza . . . just like other respiratory viral illnesses in the past, we get over this virus by achieving herd immunity. We could never achieve herd immunity by keeping the herd quarantined. It's time that we protect the vulnerable and the most at risk, but we allow the young and the healthy to open the doors and go back to work.

Do not let your voices be silenced..."[3]

MORE MUZZLING

Dr. Simone Gold, Founder of America's Frontline Doctors and an attorney, spoke up in a press conference called "White Coat Medical Summit." It went viral and then was immediately banned by all social media platforms.

Dr. Gold, along with several other doctors, were advocating for the use of hydroxychloroquine, a sixty-five-year-old FDA-approved generic drug. Hydroxychloroquine has been working on hundreds of COVID-19 patients who she and the other doctors at the press conference have been treating. What happened next was shocking.

Dr. Gold was fired for speaking up at the press conference.

Glenn Beck interviewed Dr. Gold on Blaze TV where she shared that doctors are being censored in what they can and cannot say, that there is a massive "disinformation campaign" that is costing people's lives. Dr. Gold stated that "Harvey Rich, the famous Yale epidemiologist, has estimated that 100,000 Americans would be alive today if we didn't have this massive disinformation campaign."

The Church is supposed to bring the solution—the love of Jesus—to the masses. Yet we have for the most part conformed like well-trained mice, muzzled and masked while we "shelter in place" as our cities are ravaged, our small businesses destroyed, our culture torn apart over police brutality and racism, and our nation plunged into near-irreparable debt. Furthermore, we have tyrannical governors like Virginia's Ralph Northam and California's Gavin Newsome threatening to permanently shut down churches if they gather.

But what if all this was planned—carefully engineered over decades—with a deep-state regime poised to pounce on events, like George Floyd's tragic death to fracture our culture?

What if COVID-19 is a Trojan Horse designed to destroy countries from within, collapsing economies and moving the nations toward a one-world government?

What if the U.S. politicians, who many of us have wholeheartedly supported, turned out to be part of a sinister movement? Could we Christians handle finding out the truth? [See "Dethroning The Deep State Prayer" at the end of this book.]

Better put, is our faith in Jesus stronger than our faith in "political saviors"?

> IS OUR FAITH IN JESUS STRONGER THAN OUR FAITH IN "POLITICAL SAVIORS"?

THE POLITICAL "ELITE" AND COMMUNISM

On January 10, 1963, a very concerned Florida Representative, the Honorable A.S. Herlong, read before Congress the "Current Communist Goals." Mrs. Patricia Nordman had uncovered and published these goals to alert America to the dangers of communism.[4]

I'll highlight a few of them, but you can see the complete eye-popping list in the Appendix at the back of this book. Let's see if any of these communist goals ring a bell today.

Remember, we are outlining how we got to the place of destruction in America today. I have put my sarcastic [but true] remarks in brackets following some of the listed goals.

From *The Naked Communist* by Cleon Skousen

CURRENT COMMUNIST GOALS

3. Develop the illusion that total disarmament [by] the United States would be a demonstration of moral strength.

[Hmm . . . sounds like the Democratic platform stance on our Second Amendment rights!]

4. Permit free trade between all nations regardless of Communist affiliation and regardless of whether or not items could be used for war.

[Ever get sick of the "Made in China" labels on *everything* you buy here in America when you know that China uses child labor,[5] and adult Americans need work?]

11. Promote the U.N. as the only hope for mankind. If its charter is rewritten, demand that it be set up as a one-world government with its own independent armed forces. (Some Communist leaders believe the world can be taken over as easily by the U.N. as by Moscow. Sometimes these two centers compete with each other as they are now doing in the Congo.)

[Wow. Sounds like the Antichrist wrote this one to create his one-world government "throne."]

12. Resist any attempt to outlaw the Communist Party.

13. Do away with all loyalty oaths.

[Well, well, well . . . the commies might turn over in their graves when we take the oath of commissioning at the end of this book!]

15. Capture one or both of the political parties in the United States.

[Hmm . . . now which one do you think the commies captured?]

17. Get control of the schools. Use them as transmission belts for socialism and current Communist propaganda. Soften the curriculum. Get control of teachers' associations. Put the party line in textbooks.

[Helllooo . . . They are after our children, and when you see my stats on millennials, you'll know they were successful.]

20. Infiltrate the press. Get control of book-review assignments, editorial writing, policymaking positions.

[No surprise here! FAKE NEWS abounds in the "lamestream" media.]

21. Gain control of key positions in radio, TV, and motion pictures.

24. Eliminate all laws governing obscenity by calling them "censorship" and a violation of free speech and free press.

25. Break down cultural standards of morality by promoting pornography and obscenity in books,

magazines, motion pictures, radio, and TV.

26. Present homosexuality, degeneracy and promiscuity as "normal, natural, healthy."

[Mission accomplished, Mr. "Naked Communist."]

27. Infiltrate the churches and replace revealed religion with "social" religion. Discredit the Bible and emphasize the need for intellectual maturity which does not need a "religious crutch."

[Sad. Anybody had enough of "social justice" in the pulpit and wondered what happened to Scripture?]

28. Eliminate prayer or any phase of religious expression in the schools on the grounds that it violates the principle of "separation of church and state."

[Accomplished.]

29. Discredit the American Constitution by calling it inadequate, old-fashioned, out of step with modern needs, a hindrance to cooperation between nations on a worldwide basis.

[Guess I don't need to tell you that the terms being used to discredit our Constitution are *a living, breathing Constitution.* Although that may sound like a good thing, it's actually saying that our Constitution is fluid and can change with the culture, which "is antithetical to the founding principles. The American colonists fought a war to free themselves from that kind of a system."[6]]

30. Discredit the American Founding Fathers. Present them as selfish aristocrats who had no concern for the "common man."

[Well, the commies found that the best way to discredit the Founding Fathers was to call all of them racist . . . which is a *lie*.]

31. Belittle all forms of American culture and discourage the teaching of American history on the ground that it was only a minor part of the "big picture." Give more emphasis to Russian history since the Communists took over.

38. Transfer some of the powers of arrest from the police to social agencies. Treat all behavioral problems as psychiatric disorders which no one but psychiatrists can understand [or treat].

[Hmm . . . is that before or after "defunding the police"?]

39. Dominate the psychiatric profession and use mental health laws as a means of gaining coercive control over those who oppose Communist goals.

40. Discredit the family as an institution. Encourage promiscuity and easy divorce.

41. Emphasize the need to raise children away from the negative influence of parents. Attribute prejudices, mental blocks and retarding of children to suppressive influence of parents.

42. Create the impression that violence and insurrection are legitimate aspects of the American tradition; that

students and special-interest groups should rise up and use ["]united force["] to solve economic, political or social problems.[7]

Well, I'd say that the "political elites" have been extremely successful at accomplishing their destructive goals—which should have us shaking in our boots at the reality of how well-engineered this "infiltration" into our schools, our educational systems, our media, our government, our businesses, our unions, our *children's minds* has been over the last four decades. The problem is that most of our children in public schools now have been so brainwashed that they would not recognize that communism is a bad thing! After all, looting, rioting, and killing seem to be the norm these days (#42 and #19 of the Current Communist Goals"), and we all know that this "violence and insurrection" are not solving anything, but rather promoting anarchy!

Of course, at the top of the list is disarming America—a biggie on the democratic platform and the first thing that's always done to overthrow a government. Lovely! Numbers 24, 25, and 26 aim at destroying our sexual morality and identity—really our God-given binary absolutes of male and female. This is why we are in this twisted culture where a child can defy parents and get "gender reassignment" surgery. It's why people in some states are getting sued and fired when they fail to address someone by their "preferred pronoun." There are now seventy-eight gender pronouns to choose from according to Google. The communists have been really good at number 26.

Even more infuriating are numbers 27 through 30—attacks

against the Church and America's Constitution. Number 27 is happening right now with pastors preaching more about social justice than repentance and righteousness. They're afraid to offend those who might be struggling with gender dysphoria, homosexuality, or abortion instead of giving them the truth of God's Word that will set them free, heal, and cleanse them and secure eternity for them in heaven. Prayer has already been banned from schools, work places, and many community meetings—so commies can check Number 28 off.

Did anybody watch any statues and monuments around the country get spray-painted with graffiti and then toppled over? Check #30. How about the Seattle "Summer of Love" and the Portland Bible and flag burning? Check #27. And ahh, of course, discredit the Constitution (#29), so we are willing putty in the hands of one-world government (#11) Antichrist elites!

And parents, you "negative influencers" (#41) you with your "discredited Bibles" (#27) and "discredited families" (#40). You are ruining your children with your love, faith, patriotism, and respect!

As if communism was not enough for America to be combatting, there's another sinister plan that's been implemented paralleling and intertwining with communism for the last five decades.

SOME HARD FACTS

Every Christian needs to know the rules of engagement both for Conservatives and Liberals. The left in America has been playing by Saul Alinsky's rules for a long time, and most Conservatives and Christians have been clueless as to where all the chaos came from!

THE LEFT IN AMERICA HAS BEEN PLAYING BY SAUL ALINSKY'S RULES FOR A LONG TIME, AND MOST CONSERVATIVES AND CHRISTIANS HAVE BEEN CLUELESS AS TO WHERE ALL THE CHAOS CAME FROM!

But there are a few names that are not clueless and actually adoringly subscribe to the late Alinsky's rules: Hillary Clinton and Barack Obama. Clinton knew Alinsky well. She worked with him and even wrote him a letter in 1971, begging for his new book, *Rules for Radicals*. She told Saul that he is "being rediscovered again as the New Left-type politicos are finally beginning to think seriously about the hard work and mechanics of [community] organizing."[8]

"Obama's mentors from his Chicago days studied at a school Alinsky founded, and they taught their students the philosophy and methods of one of the first 'community organizers.'"[9] Alinsky's son praised Obama in a letter he wrote to the *Boston Globe* following the 2008 Democrat National Convention: "Barack Obama's training in Chicago by the great community organizers is showing its effectiveness. It is an amazingly powerful format, and the method of my late father always works to get the message out and get the supporters on board. When executed meticulously and thoughtfully, it is a powerful strategy for initiating change and making it really happen. Obama learned his lesson well."[10]

According to an Investor Business Daily editorial,

Obama first learned Alinsky's rules in the 1980's, when Alinskyite radicals with the Chicago-based Alinsky group Gamaliel Foundation recruited, hired, trained and paid [Obama] as a community organizer in South Side Chicago. . . . In 1988, Obama even wrote a chapter for the book After Alinsky: Community Organizing in Illinois . . . [He] traveled to Los Angeles for eight days of intense training at Alinsky's Industrial Areas Foundation. . . . In turn, he trained other community organizers in Alinsky agitation tactics.[11]

So what are these rules for radicals that Alinksy crafted?" There are thirteen:

- Rule 1: *Power is not only what you have, but what the enemy thinks you have.* If your organization is small, hide your numbers in the dark and raise a din that will make everyone think you have many more people than you do.
- Rule 2: *Never go outside the experience of your people.* The result is confusion, fear, and retreat.
- Rule 3: *Whenever possible, go outside the experience of the enemy.* Here you want to cause confusion, fear, and retreat.
- Rule 4: *Make the enemy live up to their own book of rules.* "You can kill them with this, for they can no more obey their own rules than the Christian church can live up to Christianity."
- Rule 5: *Ridicule is man's most potent weapon.* It's hard to

counterattack ridicule, and it infuriates the opposition, which then reacts to your advantage.

- Rule 6: *A good tactic is one that your people enjoy.* "If your people aren't having a ball doing it, there is something very wrong with the tactic."
- Rule 7: *A tactic that drags on for too long becomes a drag.* Commitment may become ritualistic as people turn to other issues.
- Rule 8: *Keep the pressure on.* Use different tactics and actions and use all events of the period for your purpose. "The major premise for tactics is the development of operations that will maintain a constant pressure upon the opposition. It is this that will cause the opposition to react to your advantage."
- Rule 9: *The threat is usually more terrifying than the thing itself.*
- Rule 10: *The major premise for tactics is the development of operations that will maintain a constant pressure upon the opposition.* Unceasing pressure results in reactions that are essential for the success of the community organizer's campaign.
- Rule 11: *If you push a negative hard enough, it will push through and become a positive.* Every positive has its negative.
- Rule 12: *The price of a successful attack is a constructive alternative.* Avoid being trapped by an opponent or an interviewer who says, "Okay, what would you do?"
- Rule 13: *Pick the target, freeze it, personalize it, and polarize it.* Don't try to attack abstract corporations or

bureaucracies. Identify a responsible individual. Ignore attempts to shift or spread the blame.

According to Alinsky, the main job of the organizer is to bait an opponent into reacting. "The enemy properly goaded and guided in his reaction will be your major strength."[12]

Can you guess to whom Alinsky dedicated these thirteen sinister rules? If not, then the following might clue you in:

Lest we forget at least an over-the-shoulder acknowledgment to the very first radical: from all our legends, mythology, and history (and who is to know where mythology leaves off and history begins—or which is which), the first radical known to man who rebelled against the establishment and did it so effectively that he at least won his own kingdom—Lucifer.

~Saul Alinsky[13]

That's right. Alinsky dedicated his book *Rules for Radicals* to Lucifer—also known as Satan, the father of lies, the devil. And by the way, the "kingdom" Alinsky refers to is the kingdom of hell. Personally, I prefer the kingdom of heaven.

Choose this day whom you will serve . . . As for me and my house, we will serve The Lord (Joshua 24:15).

Now do you see the need for *Christian* prayer, prayer that empowers Christians in all seven mountains of culture (religion, family, education, government, media, arts and entertainment, and business) to push back the powers of darkness and preserve our country?

ONE REQUIREMENT FOR BATTLE

Only Jesus, who was fully God and fully man, the Prince of Peace, has conquered Satan by shedding his own sinless blood on the cross as a sacrifice for our sins so that we are no longer slaves to Satan. Jesus took the keys to death, hell, and the grave so that those of us who believe in Him would not perish but have everlasting life (John 3:16).

I choose life, not death. I choose the Prince of Peace, not the god of jihad.

SALVATION PRAYER

If you have never made a decision to choose Jesus as your Lord and Savior, stop right now and pray this simple prayer out loud:

Father,

According to your Word, I confess with my mouth and believe in my heart that Jesus paid the price for my sins upon the cross and was raised from the dead for my salvation.[14] Please forgive me of all of my sins, cleanse me of all unrighteous deeds with your sinless blood, and come into my heart right now. I renounce my old life with Satan, the father of lies, and declare that I am a new creation in Christ Jesus.[15] In Jesus's name, amen.

That's it. If you prayed this prayer of salvation, please visit my website DonicaHudson.com so that I may get to know you and share more spiritual growth tools with you.

There's nothing you can do to make yourself holy enough nor good enough to get into heaven. You see, the penalty of sin is death.[16] For all have sinned and fall short of the glory of God,[17] but we are saved by grace through faith. And that not of our own doing; it is the gift of God, not a result of works, so that no one may boast.[18]

As believers, you and I will live eternally with Christ Jesus in heaven because He paid the price of sin for us. Therefore, we have met the requirement for battle as we'll discuss more in Chapter 6. When we battle, we come in the name of the Lord.

Blood-bought believers in Christ must understand that this is a spiritual battle for the soul of America!

Satan has already won this battle if the Church continues to believe that the current battle for our nation is a political one and subscribes to the false narrative of separation of Church and State. In Chapter 3, "How We Got Here," I address this in detail.

> BLOOD-BOUGHT BELIEVERS IN CHRIST MUST UNDERSTAND THIS IS A SPIRITUAL BATTLE FOR THE SOUL OF AMERICA!

The days of church pastors staying silent about politics to keep butts in seats and to avoid division is borderline sin when pastors have been given the divine responsibility to protect and to guide the sheep. I'm not talking about politics. I'm talking about teaching people to vote according to biblical values.

Pastors, what will happen when judgment comes down and

those in whom your flock put their trust are jailed? They will be disillusioned, confused, and tempted to blame God.

Pastors, you must speak the truth in love concerning biblical standards of righteousness no matter what party, what state, what year. No party is perfect, and no politician is perfect. However, God's Word is true, and His ways are unchanging. There

THE TRUTH IS, ONLY THE CHURCH CAN WIN THIS BATTLE.

are certain issues that are non-negotiables with God's Word—supporting Israel, honoring marriage and the family, defending freedom of religion, opposing abortion, destroying slavery, and opposing and stopping human trafficking.

The truth is, *only the Church can win this battle.*

> *For* **we do not wrestle against flesh and blood, but against the rulers, against the authorities, against the cosmic powers over this present darkness, against the spiritual forces of evil in the heavenly places** *(Ephesians 6:12 ESV).*

It is the cosmic battle—the unseen battle between forces of good and evil–that only believers in Jesus Christ, who bear the spiritual covenant mark afforded by Jesus's shed blood, can win. You are going to be so bolstered in your faith when you read about how you are marked with the greatest authority on Earth because of your covenantal faith in Jesus (Chapter 5).

It's time for *we the people* who are the Church to speak up and step up to bat for those believers who are being annihilated by the left.

A perfect example of Alinsky-prescribed outright satanic

attack is the repetitive legal assaults against Masterpiece Cakeshop owner Jack Phillips. I observed Jack Phillips's humble and peaceful demeanor in person during an interview at Council for National Policy. Not only is Phillips being sued a third time for refusing to make a cake that conflicted with his religious beliefs, but Phillips has been satanically harassed beyond belief!

"In late September 2017, someone emailed Phillips asking for a custom cake 'to celebrate Satan's birthday,' requesting red and black icing, an upside down cross under Lucifer's head on the cake. . . . A few days later, someone called Phillips asking for a similar custom cake. . . . The caller asked Phillips to create a 'birthday' cake for Satan. . . . That the cake feature a red and black theme and an image of Satan smoking marijuana."[19]

It gets worse. "On June 4, 2018, the day that the Supreme Court issued its Masterpiece decision [siding with Phillips], someone emailed Phillips claiming to be a 'member of the Church of Satan.' That person asked for the following cake: 'I'm thinking a three-tiered white cake. Cheesecake frosting. And the topper should be a large figure of Sataan licking a 9" black Dildo. I would like the dildo to be an actual working model, that can be turned on before we unveil the cake. I can provide it for you if you don't have the means to procure one yourself.'"[20]

This is what Christians like Jack Phillips are enduring under Saul Alinsky's *Rules for Radicals*. It's so disgusting that I almost didn't include it, but I decided that covering up the persecution that's happening is part of the problem. This is absolutely enraging. Now Phillips is having to fight another legal battle marking his tenth year of persecution for carrying out his deeply held religious convictions.

Alinsky's guidelines call for conflict, ridiculing to infuriate (Rule #5), causing confusion, fear, and retreat (Rule #3), terrifying with threats (Rule #9), targeting an individual (Rule #13), putting constant pressure on that individual (Rule #8), deceitful hiding of numbers *in the dark*, and raising a din that will make everyone think you have many more people than you do (Rule #1). This is what's been done to Jack Phillips (and to President Trump continually), and it's pure evil! Christians are called to be *the light*! We are called and empowered by the Holy Spirit to boldly share truth in love that brings clarity, not confusion, courage, not fear, and peace, not rioting. Just like Jesus, we are called to be salt and light.

Today, hatred and bitterness are at an all-time high, thanks to the Satanic Alinskyites and a divided predominantly apathetic Church.

Lest you think these devilish *Rules for Radicals* are only followed by a few, be informed that when I googled "activism" in 2020, Alinsky and his rules were listed in the first pop-up pull-down, along with a tab for how much activists are paid!

During the 2016 Charlotte Riots, my good friend Bishop Larry Jackson shared with me his experience of being on a plane flying to Charlotte with a paid activist. The activist told Bishop Jackson that he often didn't know what city he was flying into, that he just did what they told him to do. This is *not* activism; this is paid criminal behavior when a person is given money to fly into a city to incite and participate in rioting, looting, property destruction, and chaos that leads to death. We need laws to prevent this!

You can hear Bishop Jackson share this story in my interview with him, "Blessing Abortion Clinics,"[21] on my website DonicaHudson.com. My guess is that these so-called "clergy" who are blessing abortion clinics are paid actors and actresses as well.

This video interview is another way that we Christians can get truth out to the world and expose the evil practices, such as paid rioters, that our own legislators may be unaware of. This is an interview with influential pastors in the Charlotte Metro area. It includes Bishop Jackson, Dr. Jim Logan, Pastor Donna Wise, and Pastor and former Congressional Candidate Leon Threatt, alongside of whom I have spoken at multiple rallies for issues that were infringing upon our religious liberties. Pastor Threatt helped organize the Clergy Prayer Vigil in the middle of the 2016 Charlotte Riots and Clergy Roundtables with President-elect Trump and with Eric and Lara Trump, in which I participated.

Seeing the pastors of the city walking the streets during the Charlotte Riots and sharing the love of Jesus was incredible. Additionally, a beautiful community relationship was born out of this chaos when my friend Cindy Decker met with then-Police Chief Kerr Putney of the Charlotte-Mecklenburg Police Department (CMPD) after the shooting death of Keith Lamont Scott. Together, they created a program called CMPD Ambassadors. The program has a series of trainings that give community members tools to build bridges across diverse communities, develop communication and conflict resolution skills and mediation tactics, and provide an understanding of local government.

Over 450 residents serve the Charlotte Community as CMPD Ambassadors. They learn Charlotte's rich history and serve as excellent hosts alongside CMPD for major sports events and conventions. These ambassadors also serve as an extra sets of eyes and ears during protests. To hear my interview with Cindy titled "Saving

Charlotte, NC . . . What you can do!" visit the video page of my website DonicaHudson.com.[22]

What the devil has meant for evil destruction, God will turn and use for good when those who are called according to His purposes rise up (Genesis 50:20)!

After Roundtable Discussion with Eric & Lara Trump 9.28.16

AT THE ROUNDTABLE WITH ERIC AND LARA TRUMP—SEPTEMBER 28, 2016

President-elect Donald Trump saw the destruction of our cities. In classic Trump fashion, he sent his trusted "A-team" in to assess the situation and come up with real-time solutions. Trump asked for *the clergy in Charlotte* to meet his son and daughter-in-law, Eric and Lara Trump.

Can you name a time in modern history when a president-elect asked the Church to meet and provide solutions in various cities? Trump also sought to help Chicago, Portland, Seattle, and other cities being ravaged by murder and riots.

I had a conversation with Eric Trump where I shared Bishop Jackson's story about the paid activists who were flying into Charlotte to riot. I also shared about the lawsuit my husband and I had brought against the Department of Justice and the Department of Education.

I showed him and Lara the letter that Obama had sent through the Department of Education to *all* public schools trying to force access for transgenders in bathrooms, locker rooms, and showers with members of the opposite biological sex even though private facilities were already provided under Title IX. This letter was an illegal effort to circumvent our nations lawmaking process, and it endangered our kids.

As I sat there at the roundtable with the Trumps, I knew deep in my heart that Donald Trump was going to win the 2016 election and that God was going to use him and his strong family to bring justice to our nation. I felt a strong urge to pray protection

Bonnie Chavda, Donica and others praying with
Eric and Lara Trump after Roundtable during the Charlotte Riots

over Eric and Lara. None of us knew at that time the historically unprecedented and relentless assaults that Donald Trump would endure and still continues to endure.

After the roundtable, Pastor Bonnie Chavda, Pastor Threatt, and I were able to pray for Eric and Lara. They are an amazing couple, and it has thrilled me to see through social media the way God has blessed them with two beautiful children since then as they serve our country faithfully.

Children are a gift from God (Psalm 127:3).

Left to Right: Donica Hudson, Leon Threatt, Betty & James Robison, Donald Trump, Frank Turek at CLERGY ROUNDTABLE Oct. 14, 2016

AT THE CLERGY ROUNDTABLE WITH DONALD TRUMP— OCTOBER 14, 2016

Again, I was amazed at how Donald Trump cared enough about the Church to call for a *clergy* roundtable. Skeptics claimed that Trump only wanted the evangelical vote.

My response is that Trump's actions from 2016 to 2020 in office have proven otherwise. He had made good on his promises toward the Church, and he had:

- Appointed two pro-life Supreme Court justices
- Created an interagency task force to combat and monitor human trafficking

- Rescued thousands from human trafficking
- Reformed our prisons
- Moved the U.S. Embassy, recognizing Jerusalem as the capital of Israel
- Signed a peace treaty with Israel
- Created a ministerial alliance to ensure our religious liberties
- Positively changed women's lives globally through the W-GDP (Women's Global Development and Prosperity Initiative)
- Signed an executive order on Advancing International Religious Freedom
- Signed a Johnson Amendment executive order that would limit Treasury's actions against religious organizations that are engaged in political campaigns—something he promised me and others directly at the clergy roundtable

Most notably, Trump recognized God's sovereignty like Washington, Lincoln, and Reagan had. He boldly called upon God to remedy our COVID-19 pandemic in his May 7, 2020 Proclamation for a National Day of Prayer.

Additionally, Trump had:

- Doubled the child tax credit, putting $2,000.00 back into people's pockets
- Regulated tariffs and trade
- Fixed bad trade deals and negotiated some great ones
- Put $1.3 billion toward the opioid crisis
- Funded pediatric cancer research

- Built up our military
- Supported and funded veterans
- Accomplished a whole boatload of other things that the mainstream media does *not* report.

You can visit my website DonicaHudson.com to hear me talk about Trump's successes in my exposé "Christianity Today's Mark Galli thinks American Christians want all varieties of sexuality!"[23]

SPEAKING ON THE WOMEN FOR TRUMP BUS TOUR—OCTOBER/NOVEMBER 2016

I met the amazing Nancy Schulze when she and I were both speaking at Gordon Conwell for the Charlotte Christian Chamber of Commerce. Nancy is a power to be reckoned with, not just because she's brilliant, bold, and beautiful; not just because she founded the Congressional Wives Speakers Association; not just because she raised tons of money for the Trump Campaign, but because she follows the Holy Spirit. Say what?

That's right. I have seen up close and personal the success of my friend and "Washington mentor," as I call her, and it's because she prays, listens to God, and acts intentionally with wisdom from above. *That's* why her plans succeed.

In prayer, Nancy conceived the idea for a "Women for Trump" bus tour.

As she says, "After I said the amen, I phoned Debbie Meadows."

Debbie is the wife of then-North Carolina Congressman Mark Meadows, who served as President Trump's Chief of Staff.

"What do you think, Debbie?"

Debbie responded, "I'm in 110 percent."

The two women swiftly put a tour together in three weeks—a mountainous task that normally would've taken six months. It ended up being a smashing success. In fact, one of Trump's chief strategists credited the Women for Trump bus tour as being a key factor in the turning point in Trump's campaign with winning the swing state of North Carolina in 2016.

On the bus tour with Nancy and the congressional wives, what impacted me the most was the faith I found at every stop in North Carolina. People were praying in the name of Jesus, which of course was and is not seen in the media.

Debbie Meadows led our morning Bible devotionals on the bus. She is one sharp lady.

I loved seeing President-elect Trump again and meeting Vice President-elect Mike Pence and his wife Karen at rallies. I loved hearing Karen talk about Scripture in small group conversations on multiple occasions and learning that she and Mike had been in Bible studies with some of the congressional couples on the tour. I felt really good about the future of our country and still do when God-fearing Christian constitutionalists run for office.

Election year 2016 was a life-changing whirlwind for me. On the heels of suing the federal government in 2015, I found myself at roundtables with the Trumps and speaking on an intensive swing state Women for Trump bus tour with some of the savviest women I know. (You know who you are, congressional wives!)

Shortly after the election, I attended the Council for National Policy as Nancy's guest. These are the nation's top movers and shakers who happen to be strong men and women of faith. Despite the horrific atrocities affecting our nation like deep-state human trafficking, clandestine plots to remove President Trump and abolish democracy, congressional people who want to replace our Constitution with Sharia law and socialism—there's still hope in the remnant—those people of faith in all seven mountains of culture who are clear headed about America's Christian heritage and will fight to preserve it.

These are just a few of the experiences compelling me to pen this guide to radical prayer that *we the people* who are Christians, should embrace before we lose our Constitution and our right in America to practice our deeply held Judeo-Christian convictions all together.

As I see it, Jews and Christians in America have a choice before us: reformation or revolution. I choose reformation rather than a bloodbath revolution of civil war, but . . .

TIME IS SHORT.
WE MUST SAVE AMERICA
BEFORE REFORMATION
IS NO LONGER AN OPTION.

Carol Threatt, Nancy Schulze, Donica,
Debbie Meadows and Paige Brydon on the Bus Tour

Campaigning for Ted Budd for Congress Bus Tour

On tour with the WOMEN FOR TRUMP CONGRESSIONAL WIVES SPEAKERS

*Left: Speaking at Trump
National Golf Course on
WOMEN FOR TRUMP
BUS TOUR 2016*

On tour with WOMEN FOR TRUMP

Karen Pence   Donica @ Pence Rally 11.4.16

WOMEN FOR TRUMP stand with Governor & Karen Pence 11.4.16

Morning devotion w/Debbie Meadows

Backstage with Trump at NC Rally with WOMEN FOR TRUMP BUS TOUR

Left: WOMEN FOR TRUMP BUS STOP at Richard Petty Museum

Seated with WOMEN FOR TRUMP at Trump Rally

Karen Pence and Donica

CHAPTER 3

HOW WE GOT HERE

SO HOW DID WE GET HERE . . . riots, looting, murder—the threat of civil war over a deeply divided America? We lived in the greatest country on Earth, founded by Christians who crafted a constitutional form of government to ensure religious liberty, and now, we have to *fight* not to be jailed and fined for practicing our deeply held Christian convictions.

The impotence of the Church began as a slow fade.

We the people started losing our constitutional and religious freedoms when legislators and judges started falsely interpreting the "separation of Church and State" as if it were law.

SEPARATION OF CHURCH AND STATE

You see, as Christians, we have thought that all we needed to do was to put all of our attention on reaching the unsaved through the local church. Unwittingly, we have subscribed to the American mindset of separation of Church and State—totally abstaining as a whole from fighting to maintain our religious liberties.

Meanwhile, Satan has captured our country in ways that our forefathers sought to prevent.

While pastors focus on tending their sheep, the enemy is stealing the very field we think we own! If we don't employ our God-given weapons of warfare that are not carnal but mighty to the pulling down of strongholds, we will lose America as a Christian nation. And it will not be the world's fault; it will be the Church's.

Did you know that "separation of Church and State" is nowhere in our U.S. Constitution nor in any of America's founding documents? Separation of powers *is* in the Constitution; separation of Church and State is *not*.

What our Constitution actually states is that "Congress will establish no religion, or prohibit the free exercise thereof." The term "separation of Church and State" comes from Thomas Jefferson's letter to Danbury Baptists assuring them that the Church would be protected from the intrusion of the state, not vice versa! I outlined this in a devotion message I shared at the Billy Graham Evangelical Association. You can view the video "BGEA Prayer September 28, 2017" on the video tab of my website DonicaHudson.com.[1]

> SEPARATION OF POWERS IS IN THE CONSTITUTION; SEPARATION OF CHURCH AND STATE IS NOT.

The Supreme Court's removal of prayer from our public schools in 1962 was a blatant misapplication of the separation of Church and State as perceived law. Since then, America has spiraled into moral decay as this separation has continued to be touted as constitutional and misused to garner state funds and legalize every moral issue from government-funded transgender surgery in the military to abortion at birth.

So where was the Church? Why did the Church not protest and stop the removal of school prayer in 1962, when this whole misinterpretation of separation of Church and State began?

Well, "the Church" had been effectively muzzled like rabid dogs by the 1954 Johnson Amendment, a provision in the U.S. tax code established by Lyndon B. Johnson that prohibits all 501(c)(3) nonprofit organizations, including places of worship, from opposing or endorsing political candidates. For the next eight years, pastors and nonprofit Christian leaders were conditioned not to speak out politically. They were so afraid of losing their tax-exempt status, that by 1962, the Supreme Court removed school prayer with little protest from the Church.

I see this as the foundational lie that Americans bought first.

The second reason I think America is in this conundrum is because of the Ethics in Government Act passed by Congress in 1978 that was born out of the Watergate scandal. This act established the Independent Counsel statute in an effort to "stand as a bulwark against any president or senior executive branch official who dared threaten the centralized executive bureaucracy put in place by the Democratic Party majorities of the 1960s and '70s. It weakened the president's political control of that sprawling bureaucracy and strengthened Congress's hand in managing it. Ultimately, it had the effect of transforming political and policy disputes—adjudicated by the elected branches of government, and thus by the people—into legal disputes in which the people have no part."[2]

The Independent Counsel statute has essentially neutered two centuries of America's original constitutional three-branch functionality when it comes to deciding most political disputes, rendering *we the people* impotent and voiceless. Today's legislative, executive, and judicial political "branches, rather than defending their institutional interests, tend to accommodate the administrative state. The centralized executive bureaucracy has become the central feature of government, administrative rulemaking has replaced general lawmaking, and rule by bureaucrats has replaced rule by elected officials."[3]

This is extremely disturbing. It's how America got into a two-year $35 million tax-payer funded Mueller investigation that *we the people* had absolutely no say in. Prior to 1978, "Members of the elected branches would defend their institutional interests, motivated by self-interest and by differing opinions regarding the public good. In the most serious political disputes, the legislature had the constitutional power to impeach the president—in which case both sides could make their case to the public and the people could decide."[4]

It's time to return the power back to *we the people* so that America's Constitution functions in its original intent instead of allowing unelected bureaucrats to do our decision-making in court. When the Independent Counsel statute was established in 1978, "this legislation was justified on the ground that executive discretion must be subordinate to law. But that masked its political purpose, which was to insulate the permanent, unelected government from political control."[5]

Democrats weaponized the subpoena powers of Congress to try and find dirt on Trump rather than getting on with the business of running our country. The left's fake "Russia Collusion" witch hunt against President Trump, plus treasonous "Spygate" involving un-elected bureaucrats in the FBI, make Watergate look like child's play.

We see today, in the two-year Mueller investigation and its aftermath, yet another attempt to destroy an anti-estab-lishment president using a legal rather than political process of adjudication. The most notable difference between this scan-dal and Watergate is that President Trump has so far succeed-ed—largely through his relentless characterization of most of those in the media as dishonest partisans rather than objec-tive reporters—in preventing the scandals surrounding him from being defined by his enemies in legal rather than political terms.

The guardians of the status quo in the permanent gov-ernment and the media have defined past political scandals so successfully that a full and proper understanding of Watergate, for instance, is likely impossible now. It remains to be seen whether, in the end, they will succeed again today—whether the legend will again become fact, and they will print the leg-end.[6]

Wow! "... whether the legend will again become fact, and they will print the legend." Sounds sickeningly familiar to Nancy Pelosi's smear campaign tactics where she outlines how to tell a lie, gets an-other partisan media source to print the lie, and then refers back to the printed lie for verification. Visit my website video page for Truth Tellers Network or visit NC Conservatives on Facebook and view these smear campaign tactics with your own eyes![7]

Journalistic integrity is gone. What happened to the journalistic standard of gathering three sources in an effort to broadcast truth? Today's mainstream media has become the left's propaganda arm. There is no fear of repercussion for broadcasting lies. In fact, it's almost a badge of honor in the fight to overthrow all things Conservative and Christian. It's despicable and saddening. Broadcasting lies cannot be the norm. We all should live by the standard of telling the truth, Christian or not.

However, did you know that *The New York Times* and *The Washington Post* were awarded Pulitzer Prizes for their so-called coverage of the FAKE Russia collusion?[8] Perfect example of how the fake news media pulls the wool over the sheep's eyes with lies. We know that it was proven that there was no collusion.

In fact, while I was researching the Electoral College, I pulled up the following supposed "fact" that popped up first in the queue on Google.

Really? ". . . a popular vote is better than the Electoral College (for obvious reasons)." What obvious reasons? I can't find any—nor does this pull-down box offer any. This is the kind of unfounded

Google | Why is the electoral college better than popular vote? | Q

All   News   Images   Videos   Shopping   More   Settings   Tools

About 9,900,000 results (0.50 seconds)

All else equal, a **popular vote** is **better than** the **Electoral College** (for obvious reasons). And a two-round **popular vote** is **better than** a single-round plurality **popular vote**, because by requiring the winner to earn a true majority, it avoids the problem of extreme minority candidates. Mar 21, 2019

If we're abolishing the Electoral College, let's also have ranked-choice ...
https://www.vox.com/.../3/.../electoral-college-ranked-choice-voting-president-democrac...

About this result   Feedback

"fact" being reported as truth that deceitfully and subconsciously brainwashes readers. The pull-down tab on Google looks like a fact finder, only readers aren't getting facts; they're getting bias cloaked in factual appearance.

Everyone's entitled to an opinion according to our First Amendment rights. However, the author of this "answer," whose identity is concealed behind Google's big tech monopoly name, should confess that this is opinion. Does America really want the liberal cities of L.A. and New York determining our presidential elections?

No. Neither did the Founding Fathers. They feared tyranny of the majority and created a constitutional republic so that a presidential candidate would have to win broad support across the country, not just in a few heavily populated cities. This protects *all* Americans, like farmers and ranchers, who need a president to protect their interests too.

I thought of my kids searching the web for research papers and being wrongly informed that everyone believes the brilliant constitutional Electoral College created by America's Founding Fathers should be abolished "for obvious reasons." This smacks of Alinsky's devilish Rule #1—*hide your numbers in the dark and raise a din that will make everyone think you have many more people than you do.*[9] How misleading and destructive. But isn't that the point?

So back to the original question: How did we get here?

The first two reasons above stem from governmental law: the 1954 Johnson Amendment and the 1978 Ethics in Government Act. A third reason is a natural law and a spiritual law of reaping what you sow, e.g., if you plant corn, you're going reap corn. If you go around hitting people, you're going get hit back eventually. The same sowing and reaping applies with nations.

Judeo-Christian believers also understand another spiritual truth: God will bless those who bless Israel and curse those who curse Israel; and all families of the earth will be blessed through Israel.[10] Therefore, when I read Chuck Pierce's revelation, "The Election . . . A New Era!" from November 14, 2012, I knew it lined up with Scripture—America was reaping what it had sown. Pierce states,

> With President Obama's speech of mid-May 2011 endorsing the Palestinian's demand for their own state based on borders that existed before the 1967 Middle East War . . . (this returns us to the warfare dimension of that season and time in U.S. History!)[11]

So what characterized the warfare dimension of the '60s and '70s in America?

- Watergate
- Civil rights protests
- Assassination of U.S. President John F. Kennedy
- Assassination of Martin Luther King; riots followed
- Assassination of Senator Robert Kennedy
- Vietnam War/Cold War
- Vietnam protests
- Cuban Missile Crisis
- Guerilla warfare (terrorism)
- Women's rights movement/women's marches
- Counterculture movement (anti-establishment movement)

The 1960s and 1970s are considered the most tumultuous and divisive decades in world history. Notice any similarities to today? Also, think about the following list of current-day warfare combined with Saul Alinsky's *Rules for Radicals* printed in 1971.

- Mueller Investigation/Spygate
- Civil rights protests/riots
- Anaheim police shooting and protests
- Flatbush Riots
- Ferguson unrest, Ferguson and St. Louis, Missouri
- 2014 Oakland riots
- 2015 Baltimore protests
- 2016 Donald Trump Chicago rally protest
- Democracy Spring
- 2016 Sacramento riot
- 2016 Milwaukee riots
- 2016 Charlotte riots
- Anti-Trump protests
- 2016 Portland, Oregon riots
- 2017 Anti-Trump protests at the inauguration in Washington, D.C.
- Occupy Wall Street
- NATO 2012 Chicago Summit Conflict
- 2017 civil unrest at UC Berkeley as Milo Yiannopoulos was scheduled to speak on campus
- Trump supporters and counterprotestors being attacked at the 2017 March 4 Trump rally
- 2017 Berkeley protests violence when Trump supporters

and protestors clashed at "Patriot's Day Rally" for Trump
- 2017 Unite the Right rally opposing the removal of a statue of Robert E. Lee
- 2017 St. Louis protests
- 2018 Patriot Prayer where Portland police declared riot as members of alt-right Patriot Prayer group clash with left-wing antifa in downtown Portland
- 2020 Minneapolis uprising and George Floyd protests
- 2020 Seattle Capitol Hill Occupational Protest (CHOP)
- Terrorism—2011 Osama Bin Laden killed/War on ISIS
- 2012 Benghazi attack
- War in Afghanistan
- Women's rights movement/ marches
- Counterculture movement (anti-establishment movement primarily against Conservatives and Christians)
- Cancel Culture
- Women's march leaders who were arrested while disrupting the Kavanaugh Confirmation and supporting the Handmaiden protest disrupting Kavanaugh final vote
- Colorado Christian baker Jack Phillips targeted for his Christian faith
- Florist Barronelle Stutzman sued and fined for declining to arrange flowers for a same-sex ceremony

The only point missing from the comparison of warfare dimensions is "assassination." I continue to pray that this does not happen. Unfortunately, with the sheer hatred I've witnessed toward Trump and all political leaders daring to challenge the global elites, all Christians should pray daily for his safety and success as the Bible commands with "petitions, prayers, intercession and thanksgiving [being] made for all people—for kings and all those in authority, that we may live peaceful and quiet lives in all godliness and holiness."[12]

It's important to note that President Trump was the most pro-Israel U.S. President in American history. Being pro-Israel is non-negotiable for a true biblical Christian activist. Mat Staver, Chairman of Christians in Defense of Israel writes:

- America recognized Jerusalem as Israel's capital and moved our embassy to the Holy City.
- The Trump administration shut down all U.S. funding for the Palestinian Authority, which pays Palestinian terrorists to attack Israelis.
- The U.S. stopped sending millions of taxpayer dollars to UNRWA--a UN agency which incites Palestinians to hate Israel.
- America withdrew from the dangerous Iran nuclear deal.[13]

My personal feelings are that President Trump won the 2020 election by a landslide, much like Reagan did when the country was sick of lawlessness and reckless liberalism. However, I believe the election was stolen. See the introduction to "Dethroning the Deep-State Prayer" for more on this at the end of this book.

I believe God is calling America to WAKE UP and turn back to Him (2 Chronicles 7:14)—to forsake innocent bloodshed of abortion, to repent of the sins of Sodom, to embrace our foundational roots of Christianity, to support Israel's sovereignty as a nation, and to seek Him once again.

There's a danger in thinking God's just going take care of this, and I can sit back on my laurels. How many more New York legislatures cheering infanticide and rainbow White Houses can a Holy God stomach?

I have a holy fear of abdicating my Christian civic responsibility. I intend to do all I can in my sphere of influence to ensure victory for candidates who govern with a biblical worldview congruent with America's Founding Fathers and our U.S. Constitution.

And finally, my last bit of revelation on the question of how did we get here?

Elaine Funderburk and Donica at Franklin Graham's Prayer Rally at Raleigh, NC Capital.

Leading Devotions at Billy Graham Library for BGEA

GREAT CULTURAL REVERSAL

During the last two-thirds of the nineteenth century, American society generally was casting aside the Christian principles on which it had been founded. Every area of American life was affected by this shift.[14] "This departure of Christians from society is known as the great 'cultural reversal,' a paradigm shift that led Christians to withdraw from the world and retreat into 'spiritual enclaves.' Today, we desperately need another paradigm shift that will spur Christians to once again occupy the spheres of influence until Jesus returns."[15]

A key leader and respected strategic thinker who's doing this well is Lance Wallnau. Lance and I did a cobroadcast at the 2016 Trump Rally in Charlotte, North Carolina. I love Lance's humor as he addresses and exposes some of the gravest issues in American history all the while being a voice of clarity and faith.

The line that hit me the most in Lance's book, *God's Chaos Candidate*, was what Trump said in a roundtable that Lance attended in 2016:

> *Every other ideaological group in the country has a voice. If you don't mind me saying so, YOU GUYS HAVE GOTTEN SOFT.*[16]

Lance goes on to surmise that "Christians are living in fear of backlash for having opinions."[17]

He's spot on . . . unfortunately.

And that, my dear friends, is absolutely and tragically how we got here.

2016 Trump Rally Co-Broadcast with LanceWallnau, Charlotte, NC

CHAPTER 4

SUPERNATURAL MANDATE

I WAS TERRIFIED AND IN AWE at the same time as I experienced a mind-blowing dream that provided the key to prayer in this book.

The dream began while I was asleep and continued as I entered into consciousness. The angelic being before me was majestic, powerful, and extremely tall. He had a square jaw, warrior athletic build with a sash around his waist, and a massive saber-like curved sword that extended from his waist to the floor. The sword alone must have been six feet long. A holy fear ran through me.

I squinted and reopened my eyes several times. Surely this wasn't real.

But it was.

This newfound holy fear was accompanied by the familiar awe-inspiring presence of the Lord, the presence of the Lord that I am addicted to when I worship and burdens leave because they are replaced by a supernatural calm and peace; that presence that envelops me when I read the Bible, when I sit down to hear and write

His prophetic words to me and to a hurting world that needs His sacrificial love so very much.

As I wrote this story, tears streamed down my face.... His Presence brings the fullness of joy and a burden for the lost simultaneously.

Yet this was a new experience. I had never encountered an angel before. And this one was clearly a warrior angel of high rank, judging by his height, buff build, and the size of his sword. His head was near the top of my ten-foot tray ceiling.

He looked straight ahead much like a soldier, yet his authority in the Spirit was almost tangible. A voice spoke to me from over the angel's right shoulder. I couldn't see from where the voice came, but I knew that it was the Holy Spirit speaking to me on behalf of the angel.

The voice introduced me to my angel named "Nikkos." (I later learned that Nikkos means "victory for the people" as does my middle name, Nicole.) His name was written in the air as the Holy Spirit spoke. I thought it odd that Nikkos had two "k's."

The voice of the Holy Spirit then shared many directives and events with me that went straight into my soul. The only way I can describe what happened was like Ezekiel when he ate the scroll (Ezekiel 3:3). I "absorbed" His words to me, which lined up with the holy Scriptures. The words concerned God's Kingdom and America. The writing of this book is the fulfillment of one of those directives.

The Holy Spirit then gave me the most profound divine instruction:

YOU ARE TO PRAY THIRD-HEAVEN PRAYERS!

I knew immediately that those third-heaven prayers will activate the angel armies, that this was a key to winning the battle over America.

But there was a problem: I had no clue how to pray these third-heaven prayers.

And what was the third heaven anyway?

There was only one place to go to find out—God's final authority, His Word (John 1:1).

THE HOLY SPIRIT THEN GAVE ME THE MOST PROFOUND DIVINE INSTRUCTION: YOU ARE TO PRAY THIRD-HEAVEN PRAYERS!

SEARCHING IT OUT

Even if it's painfully difficult, obedience feels good when your goal is to please your Creator. I was excited—like in the movies on a quest for the "Holy Grail." Psalm 25:2 kept coming to mind, "It is the glory of God to conceal a matter; to search out a matter is the glory of kings."

I don't know about you, but I want to be a "king" in God's Kingdom. That's what praying third-heaven prayers yields[1]—kingly authority to carry out God's plans on Earth as they are being carried out in heaven.

If that verbiage sounds familiar, it's because that's exactly how Jesus instructed us to pray the Lord's Prayer: ". . . Your kingdom come, Your will be done, on Earth as it is in heaven.[2] That's a third-heaven prayer.

THE THREE HEAVENS

According to Scripture, the first heaven is the realm we live in now and that we can see with our natural eyes. It contains the sun, the moon, and the stars. The second heaven is where Satan rules his evil empire of fallen angels and legions of demons.

The third heaven is where we will live eternally with Jesus and the angels with no more tears, no more sorrow nor pain. It's where there is no more need of the sun because Jesus is the light (Revelation 21:23), where we have eternal mansions (John 14:2) and walk streets of gold (Revelation 21:21) in paradise.

In Luke 23:42–43 during the crucifixion, the thief on the cross next to Jesus's cross tells Jesus, "Remember me when You come into Your Kingdom!" And He [Jesus] replies, "Truly I say to you, today you shall be with Me in paradise."

The Apostle Paul wrote, "I know a person in Christ who fourteen years ago was caught up to the third heaven—whether in the body or out of the body I do not know; God knows" (2 Corinthians 12:2–4).

CHRISTIANS ARE DUAL CITIZENS

The Bible states that followers of Christ are dual citizens. We are citizens of the Kingdom of God by faith in Jesus Christ (Philippians 3:20). We are also citizens of an earthly "kingdom." Consequently, we have obligations in both realms. Jesus commanded: "Give to Caesar what is Caesar's and to God what is God's" (Matthew 22:21).

As citizens of God's Kingdom, we are to serve Jesus above all others as the King of kings. As citizens of America, we are to submit to the civil government and obey the just laws of the land as a positive witness (1 Peter 2:15–17; Romans 13:1–7). If the laws of the two kingdoms come into clear conflict, then as Peter and the apostles put it: "We must obey God rather than men" (Acts 5:29).

Our allegiance is first, last, and always to Christ and His Kingdom, but we also have a responsibility as citizens of our nation.[3]

CHRISTIANS HAVE DUAL COMMISSIONS

Not only do we have a dual citizenship, but we have been given dual commissions. Most Christians know about the "Great Commission" to take the Good News about Jesus to everyone everywhere and to help those who receive the message become fully devoted followers of Christ (Matthew 28:18-20; Acts 1:8, etc). Fewer believers are aware of the "Cultural Commission," which is the practical application of the first instructions God gave humankind. God said, "Let us make man in our image, in our likeness, and let them have dominion over . . . all the earth. . . . God blessed them and said to them, 'Be fruitful and multiply; fill the earth and subdue it . . .'" (Genesis 1:26, 28). From the beginning, God delegated the development of culture and society to humankind.[4]

CHRISTIANS HAVE DUAL COMMANDMENTS

In addition to dual citizenship and dual commissions, Jesus also gave us two Great Commandments: love God with all our heart, soul, and mind, and love our neighbor as ourselves (Matthew 22:37–40). If we love God and love our neighbor, we will take seriously our dual citizenship and the dual commissions. Loving our neighbor certainly includes sharing the Good News, but it also means that we will actively promote the common good in the context of our community, state, and nation.[5]

It's really important to recognize that many of our public servants are carrying out their Christian civic duty under God's direction just as much as pastors of churches. After my God-encounter mandate to pray third-heaven prayers, I was invited to pray personally with two of my state's highest officials in their private chambers at the North Carolina Legislature. They were facing extreme pressure to compromise during a very heated political battle. We had a powerful time of intercession, and then I shared with them what God impressed me to say:

> *"Legislate on Earth as it is being legislated in heaven"* *(Matthew 6:20).*

Simple right? If politicians can filter all issues through this simple third-heaven concept, confusion will disappear. Legislating God's will on Earth may come with persecution, as it has to North Carolina Democrat Senator Don Davis, but the rewards are eternal! Davis cast the tie-breaking vote to override North Carolina Democrat Governor Roy Cooper's veto of the legislation directing doctors and nurses to care for an infant born alive after an attempted abortion. Senator Davis has taken *a lot* of heat and threats of unseating him in the next election for not voting with his party for infanticide.

I wrote Senator Davis an email of encouragement, thanking him for standing for life. I told him that I know it's tough to break with party lines, but God is with him when it comes to standing for the unborn, and in this case, the "born alive." I explained that I'd had the privilege and honor of leading prayer at the North Carolina General Assembly Chapel several times and in private chambers. Then I told him about the Lord clearly speaking to me to share one message in the private chambers: legislate on Earth as it is in heaven. When you do this, the force of heaven is with you. Senator Davis has the force of heaven backing him up on this one! And if God is for you, who can be against you (Romans 8:31)?

As Christians, we are ambassadors of heaven. It's not about supporting a Democratic Party or a Republican Party. It's about advocating for biblical truth on Earth regardless of party lines. Infanticide does *not* exist in heaven, and it should *not* exist on Earth.

We know that God hates hands who shed innocent blood.[6] Representative Davis's hands are clean. I'm so thankful for his strong godly stand for life and for those who share similar beliefs, no matter what party label they wear.

When the righteous are in authority, the people rejoice; but when the wicked rule, the people groan (Proverbs 29:2).

> AS CHRISTIANS, WE ARE AMBASSADORS OF HEAVEN. IT'S NOT ABOUT SUPPORTING A DEMOCRATIC PARTY OR A REPUBLICAN PARTY. IT'S ABOUT ADVOCATING FOR BIBLICAL TRUTH ON EARTH REGARDLESS OF PARTY LINES.

When we consider the totality of Scripture concerning our dual citizenship, dual commissions, and our dual commandments, it becomes apparent that it is the civic duty of all Christians to become civic activists on some level. That doesn't mean you have to speak and be out front any more than it means you have to be a pastor in the pulpit because you're a Christian. There are many ways you can fulfill your civic duty as a Christian.

WHAT THIRD-HEAVEN PRAYERS DO

In exasperation, I've heard many Christians exclaim, "We just need revival to come to America and take care of all this mess."

I agree that revival is coming and that we should pray for it. I hosted a TV show on revival for five years and hosted a 1 Chronicles 7:14 Prayer Vigil in downtown Charlotte on the first anniversary of September 11 covered by the local Fox News. I'm all about calling solemn assemblies. I've called and led many myself and still do. And yes, these prayer events work great for the short term. But for the long term, we must *create an infrastructure to sustain revival.*

The good news is that third-heaven prayers can do both. They can bring revival, and they can reform to create infrastructure in Church and State to sustain revival.

UNDOING THE WORKS OF HELL

We must be aware of how God is working right now. As Lance Wallnau points out in a video on his YouTube channel with regard to Trump as a type of Cyrus leader

". . . the church doesn't understand that God's not answering its prayers in the form of revival and awakening. . . . He's raising up secular leaders to undo the works of hell. . . . This is an important update. The average religious person's mind explodes at the thought. . . . I'm prayin' for God. . . . I'm prayin' for revival . . . You've got Nazi Germany moving on the march—God's not giving you a Smith Wigglesworth service in downtown London; He's sending Churchill.! [Trump]. . . . Derek Prince was praying in the campaign of North Africa. He was praying for God to give the victory. . . . And God says, "Stop praying for victory. I can't just arbitrarily give you victory. . . . Pray that I give you leaders such as are consistent with My glory to give you victory." In other words, I can't just arbitrarily give you something; I have to have the vessel that corresponds with My will so that I can work My will on Earth.[7]

God used President Trump to reform our government, get rid of corruption, and stop the persecution of Christians, Jews, and Conservatives so that when God does answer all of our prayers for revival—and when God does fulfill all of the prophetic words from the prophets about the billion-soul harvest—that revival is *sustained* and not snuffed out.

Let's look at the early Church. The early Church didn't need to pray for revival—they lived it for 325 years! Essentially, the government intruded upon the Church via Constantine's Council of Nicea about 325 A.D. It forced its restructuring, causing paganism to so intertwine with Christianity that the Holy Spirit departed from the Church.[8]

By 500 A.D., many church leaders were unbelievers. By the Middle Ages, church members were not even allowed to read the Bible. They didn't know Jesus loved them, let alone that He had given spiritual gifts to mankind (Ephesians 4) and how to experience the power of God.[9]

God has designed his five-fold Ephesians 4 Church to sustain the fullness of the Holy Spirit, which in New Testament terms resembles what we today call "revival." America's Founding Fathers specifically designed our Constitution to protect our religious freedoms so that the Church would be free to operate in full compliance with the Bible without fear of government intrusion.

We the people who *are* the Church need to occupy offices on all seven mountains of culture—government, church, media, business, arts and entertainment, education, and family. We must reclaim lost religious freedoms and create legislation to protect us in the future. We must see the Johnson Amendment repealed so that the Church regains her voice, see abortion ended, see prayer reinstated in schools, and much more.

All American Christians today should pray and be active in the political mountain. With the threat of losing our republic to socialism, Sharia law, deep-state globalists, and liberal organizations that want to ban God from the public square, it's ignorant to think we can continue worshipping on Sundays as normal and not publicly support and advocate for the preservation of our religious freedoms. If we continue this mindset, we will lose the privilege of worshipping freely on Sundays as Christians—pandemic or not!

It's an abdication of our Christian civic duty to think that simply praying for revival is *all* we need to do to save America.

I'll admit it can be overwhelming to look at the extreme issues we are facing today, but if all we do is pray for revival, we need only look to history to see that corrupt governments can easily snuff out revival, not because governments are stronger than God, but because God's people did not fight to change the government. Activism is a must for the modern Church!

As Edmund Burke is credited with saying, "The only thing necessary for the triumph of evil is for good men to do nothing."[10]

The Church needs to embrace a cultural mind shift away from "separation of Church and State." She must engage in civic duty, which is to recognize and to work hand in hand with God-appointed "Cyruses" from outside the Church to reform government. Like Nehemiah's workers who restored the sovereign state infrastructure, we must build with one hand and hold a weapon in the other (Nehemiah 4:18). We must be active prayer warriors with our weapons of warfare that are not carnal but mighty to the pulling down of strongholds if we want to save America.

> IT'S AN ABDICATION OF OUR CHRISTIAN CIVIC DUTY TO THINK THAT SIMPLY PRAYING FOR REVIVAL IS ALL WE NEED TO DO TO SAVE AMERICA.

In admonishing Christians to pray for revival, Rabbi Jonathan Cahn warns that if America does not turn back to God, we'll get what's promised—judgment. God gives warnings but also gives windows of grace to return to Him like He did with King Josiah in the Bible.

Rabbi Cahn warned, "The [2020] election is not the answer; it's the window for the answer. In this reprieve period, if we end up having a political turning and *not* a spiritual turning, everything will proceed to judgment."[11] This begs the question: has America proceeded to judgment or will the church pray for a spiritual turning that reclaims our nation for Christ?

We must do both—pray for revival and build infrastructure to sustain it.

On the morning of February 5, 2013, I had a revival dream. In the dream, I was speaking to a group and saying, "Although we can't *plan* revival, we can *prepare*. The ten virgins who *prepared* their lamps entered into the presence of the Bridegroom. The others who did not prepare did not enter in."

Then I awoke with this realization: *prayer* is *preparation.*

God has placed within me a mandate for constitutional prayer—a call to raise up the remnant to revive the root of our constitutional freedom in America—to ensure that America the beautiful remains ONE NATION UNDER GOD, INDIVISIBLE, WITH LIBERTY AND JUSTICE FOR ALL.

CHAPTER 5

UNDERSTANDING COVENANT

WHEN OUR CREATOR GOD LOOKS upon the earth, He views us and our bloodlines through His covenants. He calls Himself the *God of Abraham, Isaac, and Jacob*. He is pointing to the Abrahamic covenant for a nation set apart for Himself and carried out through the bloodlines of Isaac and then Jacob and his descendants (Exodus 2:24; 4:5).

In Jeremiah 31:31, we see God continually renewing and restoring *but never replacing* the covenant with His people, Israel. Time and again, God reminds Israel of His civil covenant with her.[1]

The biblical term for "covenant" means a binding agreement between two parties. In Hebrew, the word "covenant" is *Berith*. In Greek, it's *diatheke*. It actually means to "cut covenant,"[2] which is cutting flesh and mingling blood.

UNDERSTANDING COVENANT TERMS

So what does Jesus mean when He says, "I am in the Father, and the

Father is in Me" (John 14:11)? What does it mean for us as believers to be "in Christ" (John 14:20)?

The answer lies in understanding covenant and covenant terms.

John 14:8–11 tells us that "Philip said to [Jesus], 'Lord, show us the Father, and it is enough for us.'"

Jesus said to him, "Have I not been with you so long, and you still do not know me, Philip? Whoever has seen me has seen the Father. How can you say, 'Show us the Father'? Do you not believe that I am in the Father and the Father in me? The words that I say to you I do not speak on my own authority, but the Father who dwells in me does his works. Believe me that I am in the Father and the Father is in me, or else believe on account of the works themselves."

WHAT DOES IT MEAN FOR US AS BELIEVERS TO BE "IN CHRIST"?

The Bible is a book about redemption. It is that or it is nothing at all.[3] God brought redemption for mankind through His covenant—the blood covenant of His only begotten Son, Jesus, who shed His sinless blood (Galatians 4:4, Romans 5:12) on the cross for the redemption of our sins (John 3:16, Isaiah 53:6). This is how we are "in Christ" as adopted sons and daughters of Christ by covenant.[4] Christians do not practice blood covenant sacrifices for sin today because Christ Jesus paid the price once and for all.

A blood covenant between two parties is the closest, the most enduring, the most solemn, and the most sacred of all contracts. It absolutely cannot be broken. When you enter into blood covenant with someone, you promise to give them your life, your

love, and your protection forever . . . 'til death do you part.
Marriage is a blood covenant. We don't honor marriage as a
blood covenant, but God says it is. (See Malachi 214; Proverbs
2:17.) . . . The blood covenant is consummated when the hymen
is broken. You see now why God says pre- and extra-marital
physical intercourse is a sin (Exodus 20:14; Matthew 5:27; 1
Corinthians 6:18; 10:8; Galatians 5:18).[5]

Understanding covenant brings much deeper meaning to the language in the Bible, such as being "in Christ" and why Jesus hung on a "tree." A great explanation on the background of Hebrew blood covenants can be found in *The Miracle of the Scarlet Thread* by Richard Booker. Booker explains the nine-step blood-covenant ritual that Hebrew males practiced in biblical times. Blood covenant was not only a Jewish thing; other nations around them also practiced them.

So what were the nine steps? (All of these are adapted from Booker's book.)

1. **Take off and exchange robes or coats.** The robe was the person's identity—the total person, so you were basically saying that "I'm giving you all of me, my being and my life." Do you remember when a girl would wear her boyfriend's letter jacket in high school? Same concept—everyone knew that girl belonged to the guy who owned the jacket—at least until they broke up, and she returned the jacket. Only in Hebrew culture, this blood covenant ritual was meant for life—'til death do you part.

2. **Exchange belts.** The belts contained the weapons and held

the armor together. The exchange meant you were saying to each other, "Here is my strength and all my ability to fight. If anybody attacks you, they are also attacking me. Your battles are my battles, and mine are yours. I will fight with you. I will help defend you and protect you."[6]

3. **Cut the Covenant.** The two Hebrew males entering into covenant would then cut an animal straight down the middle, laying each half on either side of them. They'd stand between the bloody halves with their backs to each other and then walk through the bloody halves making a figure eight and coming back to stand facing each other. This meant two things: "First, we are saying that we are dying to ourselves, giving up the rights to our partner unto death. . . . Each half of the dead animal represents us. And second, since the blood covenant is the most solemn pact, we each point down to the bloody animal split in two and say, 'God do so to me and more if I ever try to break this covenant. . . .'"[7]

4. **Raise Right Arms and Mix Blood.** Raise right arms, cut palms, and bring palms together, intermingling blood, and then swear allegiance to each other. The significance of the blood intermingling was the two becoming one.

5. **Exchange Names.** While standing with right palms together and blood intermingling, the Hebrew males took each other's last names as part of their own.

6. **Make a Scar.** The next step the Hebrew males would take is to make a scar by rubbing the blood together as a permanent testimony to the covenant. It was a constant reminder

every time they looked at their hands of their responsibilities to each other—the "guarantee of the covenant."[8] If anyone tried to harm one of the males, all they had to do was raise up the right arm and show the scar. That meant, "There's more to me than meets the eye. If you're coming after me, you're also going to have to fight my blood covenant partner."[9]

Henry Stanley, on his explorations through Africa, cut covenant 50 times with various chieftains. And we can certainly understand why. Anytime he would come across an unfriendly tribe, he would just hold up that right arm with those 50 scars and any would be attacker would take off running in the other direction.[10]

7. **Give Covenant Terms.** The males would then stand before witnesses and give the terms of the covenant, reading off their assets and liabilities. They were saying, "All my assets are yours. All my money, all my property, and all my possessions are yours. If you need any of them, you don't even have to ask. Just come and get it. What's mine is yours, and what's yours is mine. And if I die, all my children are yours by adoption, and you are responsible for my family.

8. **Eat Memorial Meal.** A memorial meal of bread representing flesh, wine representing the blood of grapes (Genesis 49:11), and life blood is eaten. The males "take a loaf of bread, break it in two, and feed it to each other saying, 'This is symbolic of my body, and I'm now put-

ting it in you.'" Then they'd serve each other wine and say, "This is symbolic of my life blood which is now your blood. . . . I'm in you, and you're in me. We are now one together with a new nature."[11]

9. **Plant a Memorial.** As a memorial to the covenant, a tree is planted and sprinkled with the blood of the animal. The blood-sprinkled tree, along with the scar, will always be a testimony to the covenant.[12]

Step 9 completes the ceremony, and the Jewish males would always be known as "friends" from that point on. In biblical times, the term "friend" was not used loosely as it is today. You became friends only after you had cut covenant. And all the children, even the unborn ones, would be included in the covenant because they were "in" them.[13]

The first time I heard this thirty years ago, I was stunned and shocked that I had not learned it earlier. I had heard all the terms of being "in Christ" but did not realize that being "in Christ" meant being with God before the foundations of the world (1 Peter 18–20) and that it is the ultimate in covenant. Booker puts it this way:

All creatures put together don't equal the Creator. So if God became man, while at the same time, remaining God, He could stand in for all creation. He could represent all mankind. All humanity would be in Him. He could take the place of every person who ever lived. And being equal to God, even though a man, He could enter into covenant with Himself on behalf of all humanity.[14]

Did you get that? The culture at the time of Jesus fully recognized the steps listed for the ceremony of blood covenant. So when Jesus offered Himself as the perfect spotless lamb for sacrifice, God was "cutting covenant" with Himself through His only begotten Son, Jesus.

Let this mind be in you which was also in Christ Jesus, who, being in the form of God, did not consider it robbery to be equal with God, but made Himself of no reputation, taking the form of bondservant, and coming in the likeness of men. And being found in appearance as a man, He humbled Himself and became obedient to the point of death, even the death of the cross. Therefore God also has highly exalted Him and given Him the name which is above every name, that at the name of Jesus every knee should bow, of those in heaven, and of those on earth, and of those under the earth, and that every tongue should confess that Jesus Christ is Lord, to the glory of God the Father (Philippians 2:5–11).

So why did I go into all this about blood covenant when this is supposed to be a book about praying for America?

If God the Father, through Jesus the Son, died for all of humanity to be redeemed, He is certainly into redeeming countries that entered into civil covenants with Him.

So what's a civil covenant, and how does it relate to praying for our nation's Constitution?

According to William Thomas Crabtree in his senior thesis on "Our Covenant-Constitution,"

> *The Constitution was not created in a vacuum; it is rather the result of thousands of years of political thought and discourse stretching "back to the Covenant tradition of the Old Testament." It is this covenant tradition that bears import for politics and governance today.*
>
> *Donald Lutz, a professor of political science at the University of Houston and preeminent scholar in the field of American Constitutionalism, describes a covenant as "a formal agreement that had legal validity under the seal of the Crown, which denoted a serious agreement witnessed by the highest authority. The counterpart to the secular covenant was any agreement secured by God." In more fundamental terms, a covenant is the "most serious type of agreement attested to, or witnessed by the highest available authority." The elements that identify it as such are: a justification of authority, continuity or limited changeability, invocation of God or the highest authority, the presence of various sanctions, and an incorporation of posterity.[15]*

COVENANTS ARE DIFFERENT FROM CONTRACTS

America has a "contract mentality" instead of a covenant understanding. In contracts, the signatories of the contract operate by "if, then . . ." type clauses with time limits. If one of the signatories breaks the contract, then the whole contract is null and void. Covenants, however, incorporate a "self-sacrificing *agape* [love] that is the basis of intimate, eternal relationships."[16] In a marriage covenant, both the man and woman give themselves totally to each other 'til death do them part, invoking God's blessing. With a contract mentality, a man and wife might think along the lines of staying married until one does something the other dislikes.

It seems ridiculous to think of the Declaration of Independence as a mere contract, yet many mistakenly do. In the civil covenant of the Declaration of Independence, the fifty-six signers all understood they were committing high treason against the British government by signing the document. Benjamin Franklin underscored the incredible danger by famously stating, "We must all hang together, or assuredly we shall hang separately."[17] Covenant denotes unity and "til death do us part" commitment. Further, covenant invokes the higher authority of God.

Note the covenantal clause of the Declaration of Independence:

"And for the support of this Declaration, with a firm reliance on the protection of divine Providence, we mutually pledge to each other our Lives, our Fortunes and our sacred Honor."

Understanding the basis of covenant versus contract will open up a security in the hearts of those who are in covenant with God. They know that God Himself will fight for us to preserve our "covenant Constitution" when He sees that the remnant people of faith are calling upon Him. That is the nature of covenant that invokes a Holy God.

The currency of covenant is LOVE.

But God commendeth His love toward us, in that, while we were yet sinners, Christ died for us (Romans 5:8).

MISUNDERSTANDING GOD IN COVENANT

I've met many folks who are so steeped in contract mentality that they think if they sin in any way, they've broken their attempted "contract" with God, so why try? Why try to be a Christian if God's out there ready to whack you every time you mess up? Preaching designed to scare people into submission doesn't help but actually reinforces a Pharisaic works-based mentality that is simply unattainable. And who'd want to be in a relationship with a God like that anyway? It is the love of God that draws man to repentance and faith (Romans 2:4).

So what did Jesus mean when He said, "Be perfect as your Heavenly Father is perfect" (Matthew 5:48)?

We know that sinless perfection is the requirement for entering heaven because Romans 3:23 tells us that all have sinned and fall short of the glory of God. Furthermore, the penalty of sin is death (Romans 6:23). And we know that we sin daily, even if it's as little as only having a fleeting sinful thought or as great as murder. So how are we supposed to be able to get to heaven?

Through the blood covenant of Jesus Christ.

Remember the Hebrew blood covenant described at the beginning of this chapter?

Jesus, "Son of God," who was fully God and fully man, without sin, exchanged names (step 5 of Booker's nine steps) with us as the "Son of Man" (John 3:16, Romans 5:12). Jesus exchanged His "robe of identity" (Step 1) for our robe of sin, literally taking the sin of mankind upon Himself on the cross. He exchanged belts (Step 2) and gave us His authority and weapons in battle (2 Corinthians 10:4, Ephesians 6:11–18).

Step 8 was fulfilled during the covenant ceremony when Jesus had the covenant meal of bread and wine with His disciples. "After the meal Jesus went out and left a memorial to the covenant. He planted a tree. And He poured out blood on it. But it wasn't a little nick in His wrist. It was all His blood poured out at the foot of the cross, the bloodstained tree that stands forever as a memorial to the covenant (Step 9). The *Lamb of God* slain from the foundations of the world cut covenant for all mankind. And we were there. We were crucified with Him. . . ."[18]

Therefore, when God looks at those of us who have chosen to take on Christ's name—Christians—by professing faith in Jesus, He does not see evil sin. He sees us as forgiven—as His children!

For you are all children of God by faith in Christ Jesus (Galatians 3:26).

But as many as received Him [Jesus], to them gave he power to become the sons of God, [even] to them that believe on his name (John 1:12).

The Spirit itself bears witness with our spirit; that we are the children of God . . . (Romans 8:16).

For as many as are led by the Spirit of God, they are the sons of God (Romans 8:14–19).

As God's covenant children, we can approach Him and ask anything in Jesus's name that we have need of and know that He will do it (John 14:14).

SEALING THE DEAL

Finally, God sends the Holy Spirit to seal the deal. When we ask Jesus to come into our hearts as believers, we are inviting the Holy Spirit to dwell within us as the seal who bears witness and testifies to the covenant (John 20:22). This is how we become one with God and acquire a supernatural scar (Step 6).

When Satan comes against us, we can show that supernatural scar. "You see, greater is He who is in us (the Holy Spirit) than he (Satan) who is in the world" (1 John 4:4). *And when Satan sees our scar, he will flee from us because he knows he has already been whipped by our blood covenant brother, Jesus Christ. . . ."*[19]

POWER IN THE BLOOD OF JESUS

The most powerful thing in the universe is Jesus's sinless blood. All of the spirit realm fears it and reveres it. It covers mankind's sins and redeems us from eternal death. It washes us white as snow. It's our ticket to paradise. It provides healing and deliverance for those who are oppressed. It reminds the devil of his doomsday in the lake of fire. It causes the enemy to flee and brings protection when we plead it over our lives, our bodies, and situations.

As Andrae Crouch's song goes, *"It reaches to the highest moun-*

tain. And it flows to the lowest valley. The blood that gives me strength from day to day. . . . It will never lose its power."[20]

JOINING THE REMNANT THAT REVIVES THE ROOT

This is why the remnant—those who are in Christ Jesus—must join together and reclaim our covenant Constitution. We have the authority to do so because we are in covenant with the same God who covenanted with our Founding Fathers of the Mayflower Compact, the Declaration of Independence, and the U.S. Constitution. This is our land, and we in the "Prayer Force of Heaven" can show our "supernatural scars" to the enemy of this land and declare that our foundational roots of civil covenant will not be destroyed but shall be revived in Jesus's name.

CHAPTER 6

BATTLE UP

"I'VE ONLY HAD a handful of the kind of experiences that I'm gonna share now," my beautiful red-haired friend Bonnie Chavda stated as I interviewed her on Zoom.

I was already on the edge of my seat because Bonnie had shared bits and pieces of her experience with me in the past, and I knew that it was a key to prayer for our country. Bonnie is one of the most anointed and brilliant women I know. She and her husband, Mahesh Chavda, have ministered globally for over thirty-five years.

Bonnie continued, "Just a few years ago in the month of July and for several weeks [afterward], I had these images of Ben Franklin just popping up in my mind. I'd look at something on the Internet or various other things, and that very classic face of Ben Franklin with his little glasses and that long hair, those little beady eyes . . . kept popping up everywhere. It was very strange, but it was happening so frequently that I started to kind of notice it.

"I was driving to our July summer conference that we do every year. On my way . . . to our church facility, I passed this huge billboard of a hundred-dollar bill with a picture of Ben Franklin on it. It was so radical because I've been seeing him so often that as I passed it, I asked out loud [to Ben Franklin] just kind of jokingly, 'Are you trying to tell me something?'

"I went on to the conference. . . . We were hosting our principal speakers Bill and Beni Johnson, who are good friends of ours. They've been absolutely darling to join us for our family conferences in July every year. At that time, Bill's PA [personal assistant] was a woman named Judy Franklin. We had dinner all together, and everyone was leaving the dining room. Judy and I were the last to leave.

"Well, a couple of years before, she and I had begun a conversation about supernatural experiences, and we didn't get to finish. . . . I was mentored by Derek Prince, and he, in my opinion, was one of the great Spirit-filled exegetical teachers of the last century. Derek was very specific about finding your revelation from Scripture.

"So anyway, I wanted to talk to Judy about some of the trends that were going on in the body of Christ at that time. I was still sitting at the table. She [Judy] turned around and came back into the room and said, 'Well, I guess now is as good a time as any to tell you.'

"I had no idea what that meant.

"She said, 'Do you know why my name is Franklin? I was married to the last living descendent of Benjamin Franklin.'

"And, of course, at that moment, God had my attention. The whole space had my attention because I had just said to Ben Franklin's face, 'Are you trying to tell me something?'

"Then she [Judy] said, 'You are connected to the Senate. No, I mean *the Senate*, and there's an angel.'

"And when she said, 'There's an angel,' (I've never had this happen before), my right side literally opened, and I could see the bottom portion of this huge angel. He had his wings folded over the front of his body covering his feet and legs. All embedded or encrusted in him were these beautiful blue and red gemstones—massive things. The colors were red, white, and blue. I knew he was some kind of a major angel assigned to God's destiny for America."

Interviewing Bonnie Chavda

MOUNT RUSHMORE, THE HEAVENLY SENATE, AND CONGRESS

"And at that moment . . . something filled me physically, this warm, wonderful something that was so heavy. It was like filling a balloon with water, and then it would roll out of the chair onto the floor. That's sort of what happened. I rolled out of my chair, and I can just tell you, I was not there anymore. My body was there, but my person—this person who's talking with you right now—was standing in front of Mount Rushmore.

"I had never been to Mount Rushmore. I wasn't a student of Mount Rushmore, so Mount Rushmore wasn't something that was frequenting my brain or my knowledge or my experience. I was standing in front of Mount Rushmore and the presidents. The stone on Washington, Jefferson, and Lincoln began to crack and fall off their faces. As it did, they all turned in the direction of the national capital and begin to repeat their own words written and spoken, their own words from our national history, all together in a chorus.

"As that was happening, I suddenly found myself in a different place. I was in this huge living rotunda. The best way I can describe it is that it was an eternal United Nations, but it was made up of believers from the very first ones in every nation who had been praying, serving the Lord, bringing people to the Lord, and understanding the national destiny of the gospel in their nation throughout its history. It was amazing!

"This thing was living!"

"It [I call it the heavenly Senate] was like huge stadium with seating going down to the center where there was the absolute brightest light, almost like an orb, but it was just the aura of this bright, bright light. In the natural, you knew that if you looked at that light, it should blind you. But you could look at that light, and when you looked at that light, you knew it was the **LAMB OF GOD—JESUS—crucified, resurrected, ascended, and seated on the throne of heaven in the center of all the nations!**"

"What would happen is this heavenly Senate would turn. I was against the wall of it, and it was vibrating with life. I understood that it would continue to grow because it was being populated by the generations of believers in their nations throughout history.

"A few rows down in front of me were individuals whom I knew personally and had gone on to be with the Lord—Derek Prince, Ruth Heflin. They understood our national destinies specifically in light of studying the history.

"So this thing—that heavenly Senate—turned on great axles that I understood were seasons of time, chronological time. (The Bible speaks often about things happening with God in the fullness of time.) It didn't just happen once. It turned on these great axles of time and stopped where the delegation of the United States was directly in front of the Lamb. There was one spokesperson in a circle, much like you read in Scripture about the elders around the Lamb's throne in Revelation. Only this was like a legislative body that was meeting now, not in the past, but a living meeting. And every nation had an individual spokesperson.

"From what I understood, these spokespersons didn't change. The U.S. came before the Lamb and stopped. The spokesperson stood up from his seat, took one step forward, and put his hand on this little square wooden lectern-like thing that was on a post. In that moment, it was like an affirmation that there was some kind of an authority. I guess it reminded me of when presidents were sworn in, they put their hand on the Bible. Anyway, he put his hand on this little wooden thing and stood in a very elegant pose.

"As he stood there—I don't know why I knew this—I understood him to be Patrick Henry. He began to speak to the Lamb in English. He didn't say his own words but a river of words that were the coming together, the condensation of the many words, prayers, declarations, written documents, and publications that all of the servants of the Lord (believers in the nation) had said during their own lifetimes. It all came together out of the spokesperson's mouth, out of Patrick Henry's mouth. In what seemed like a few seconds, Patrick Henry [spoke this] presentation. It was very short, powerful and included all the generations.

"There was no debate. No questioning. No additions. No anything.

"The Lamb, Jesus, had this huge wooden scepter, and He just lifted it up and hit it once on the floor and said, 'Amen!'

"That amen thundered out of heaven into the cosmos in a way that literally shook the entire cosmos. There's no way that anything in creation could not get shaken by that.

"For a moment, I was back in front of Mount Rushmore. All of the presidents were sending their words over to our national capital. I saw very specifically not the White House but the rotunda of the Congress. A huge lightning bolt hit the top of the Congress. I understood very clearly that it was the historical and then the heavenly cloud of witnesses agreeing with the Lamb's amen for our nation, that [it] was going to have a dramatic impact, and it wasn't about the presidency. Interestingly enough, it [that lightning strike] was about Congress.

"And in that moment, I was suspended over the nation, and I saw this high, thick cloud, this yellowish murky grayish-like thick, thick, thick air pollution smog. It was just a couple of feet above the head of your average tall man and just over the heads of the entire nation. This thick, thick smog was made up of religious voices, political voices, all kinds of media voices, divisions, anger, peoples' opinions, and all kinds of social media, a cacophony of voices.

THE LAMB'S AMEN

"The Lamb's very clear amen was on the words of our Founders, of all the believers who have understood America's calling from its very inception as a light among nations, specifically a city on a hill for the establishment and spread of the Christian gospel that is deeply ingrained in the destiny and foundation of our nation.

"When that very clear amen hit that smog, it was muffled. It went from sharp and powerful to just 'Mmmmmmmm.'

"There's a place in Scripture where Jesus is being baptized, and the Father speaks and says, 'This is My Beloved Son. Listen to Him.' And some said when God spoke this about His Son, it thundered.

"So The Lord said, '**When the believers walking around on the surface of the U.S. begin to agree with the Lamb's amen, I will break the spell off of the mindset and hearts of America!**'"

Then that was the end of this interview titled "Bonnie Chavda: Mt Rushmore, the Heavenly Senate and Congress." It is available on my website video page for Truth Tellers Network at DonicaHudson. com.[1]

What was profoundly amazing to me was the "heavenly Senate" in Bonnie's revelation. It made sense on several levels. There was a heavenly Senate of nations because Jesus's inheritance *is* the nations (Psalm 82:8, 2:8; Revelation 2:26). It also brought to mind the portion of the Lord's prayer where Jesus admonished us to pray "Your kingdom come, Your will be done, on Earth as it is in heaven." We have Senates and a United Nations on Earth, so why wouldn't there be one in heaven (Matthew 6:10)?

As I looked, "thrones were set in place, and the Ancient of Days took his seat. His clothing was as white as snow; the hair of his head was white like wool. His throne was flaming with fire, and its wheels were all ablaze (Daniel 7:9).

It's also intriguing that the Senate walls were living and had "great axles" that moved and could grow as it was populated with more believers from the nations. This reminds me of Roberts Liardon's book *We Saw Heaven* where Roberts describes a couch in heaven that "cuddled" him, writing, "It is as if comfort 'lives' in the furniture of Heaven."[2]

Equally eye-opening was that the Senate turned on axles of chronological time. The Apostle Paul greeted the saints in Ephesus by reminding them "Blessed be the God and Father of our Lord Jesus Christ, who has blessed us in Christ with every spiritual blessing *in the heavenly places*, even as he chose us in him before the foundation of the world. . . . In him we have redemption through his blood, the forgiveness of our trespasses, according to the riches of his grace, which he lavished upon us, in all wisdom and insight making known to us the mystery of his will, according to his purpose, which he set forth in Christ as a plan for the fullness of time, to unite all things in him, things in heaven and things on earth" (Ephesians 1:3–4, 7–10).

God has certainly made known a "mystery of His will" through Bonnie's revelation.

CONGRESS AND JUDGMENT

The lightning striking the rotunda of Congress is most certainly a sign of judgment (Job 36:30–33; Exodus 9:23--24). We must cover those in Congress who are righteous in prayer and pray for those who are not to repent or to be voted out of office.

After Bonnie's interview, I knew more than ever that the Founding Fathers were speaking to us through the ages from the ancient foundations of our country. Bonnie's encounter fit like a puzzle piece next to my God-encounter mandate to pray third-heaven prayers. That's how the body of Christ works.

I knew that in this book, I *must* offer prayers of agreement with the Founding Fathers and our civil covenants more than ever. This is how we "raise up the foundation of many generations" as "repairers of the breach!" (Isaiah 58:12).

For *If the foundations are destroyed, what can the righteous do (Psalm 11:3)?* And America is dangerously close to having her foundation destroyed.

Before getting into the prayers, it's important to understand how prayer works in general.

So as we pray to God in Jesus's name, who carries out these prayers?

THE ANGELIC PRAYER FORCE

Are not all angels ministering spirits sent to serve those who will inherit salvation (Hebrews 1:14)?

Praise the Lord, you his angels, you mighty ones who do his bidding, who obey his word (Psalm 103:20).

In Bonnie's encounter, the mighty angel she saw at her right side with massive gemstones of red, white, and blue obviously represented America. We know from Daniel 12:1 and 10:13 that the mighty angel Michael is one of the "chief princes" who protects Israel. It stands to reason that the United States has mighty angels protecting our nation too.

According to Colossians 1:16, angels were created by God. They have superior knowledge to mankind, and they are innumerable.

Psalms 91:11 tells us that "He will command his angels concerning you to guard you in all your ways." That means that Christians have the right to believe that God gives us at least two angels to protect us everywhere we go. (Note: "angels" is plural)

Psalms 34:7 tells us that "The angels of the Lord encamp round about those of us who fear Him. . . ." These angels deliver us from evil. These angels protect us at all times. As believers under the blood covenant of Christ Jesus, our protection is much greater than our enemies.

Like us, angels worship God.

Revelations 5:11–12 (NKJV) says, "Then I looked, and I heard the voice of many angels around the throne . . . and the number of them was ten thousand times ten thousand . . . saying with a loud voice: 'Worthy is the Lamb who was slain to receive power and riches and wisdom, And strength and honor and glory and blessing!'"

Angels also execute God's judgements. God not only judges individuals (Hebrews 9:27), but He judges nations (Psalm 110:6, Matthew 25:30, Isaiah 66).

Angels descend and ascend from the third heaven through "Satan's campground" of the second heaven to us here on Earth in the first heaven. In Daniel 10 when Daniel went into a three-week period of mourning, fasting, and prayer over a troubling vision of great war, God sent Daniel an angel to explain the vision. Daniel's angelic messenger said, "Do not be afraid, Daniel. Since the first day that you set your mind to gain understanding and to humble yourself before your God, your words were heard, and I have come in response to them. But the prince of the Persian kingdom resisted me twenty-one days. Then Michael, one of the chief princes, came to help me, because I was detained there with the king of Persia. Now I have come to explain to you what will happen to your people in the future, for the vision concerns a time yet to come" (Daniel 10:12–14).

Daniel's angelic messenger told him that he was delayed by the demon prince of Persia. This was a second-heaven battle where Michael, Israel's chief prince, came to help Daniel's angelic messenger.

All of these Scriptures and more help me to understand the angelic dream encounter I had with the mandate to pray third-heaven prayers so that God's will be done on Earth as it is in heaven. Like the Apostle Paul in 2 Corinthians 12:2–4, I too have a friend who is often caught up to heaven. At first, I found this hard to believe, but after several years of his calling me with undeniable revelations that have lined up with the Bible and with what I was experiencing at that very moment, I know that he speaks truth. And I thank God for him.

ROCKIN' AND SCROLLIN'

On one occasion, my friend gave me a scroll to write on to encourage me. He told me to read Daniel 10–12. Here are excerpts from my writing. The date was September 12, 2016.

We are in the middle of the "Charlotte Riots" which God warned me of. . . . My friend has told me many times that I am chosen for this great assignment. As I read Daniel 10:11 about Daniel's being chosen or "highly esteemed," I find myself in amazement that God would choose me! Yet in a weird way, I'm not totally caught off guard because of so many things— things my mother had said to me as a child, that she "always thought I'd be famous one day." This led me on a dead-end journey spiritually when I thought that meant I should pursue earthly fame. I wasted too many days as a young person pursuing that "fame" through modelling and acting before becoming born-again and realizing every Christian should first want to become famous in heaven like the "Hebrews 11 Hall of Faithers." Those giants of the faith extend their awards and rewards to us in baton-like fashion to help us fulfill our covenant promises (Hebrews 11:39–40) on Earth as they watch, cheer, and pray from heaven in the cloud of witnesses!

I had a seminary mentor say to me years after fleeing empty earthly pursuit of fame, that I was "famous in heaven." He stated this after I told him a story about arriving on a foreign mission field and being told at the airport by one of the indigenous leaders whom I'd never met, that he wanted me to pray for him because he knew I had this "special power from heaven." Later, this kind-hearted guy ended up getting delivered from fear, which probably entered when he was abused as a child.

I quickly learned that being "famous in heaven" often means being hated and persecuted on Earth by the religious and those who do not know Jesus. As it was with Jesus, so shall it be with us. As it was with Daniel, so shall it be with us (John 15:20)!

When did Daniel become highly esteemed or famous in heaven?

"Since the first day he set his mind to gain understanding and to humble himself before his God and his words were heard . . ." (Daniel 10:12).

Have you set your mind to gain understanding from God and humbled yourself before Him?

Once in my younger years of zeal, I encountered a Jewish guy on the beach. I naively exclaimed, "Wow! It's awesome that you're Jewish. You're one of God's chosen people!"

"Chosen to suffer," he replied from a cynical nonredemptive vantage point.

His comment can be all too true even to Spirit-filled believers who have lost hope. Yes, being famous in heaven can mean suffering on Earth, but the retirement package is out of this world and eternally secure!

I'd rather obey God here on Earth doing His will according to His Word and be hated than to live eternally in heaven with regret. My motto has always been that "I want to accomplish everything God has for me here on Earth, nothing more and nothing less. Nothing more because I do not want to bog myself down in fleshly pursuits that can be good but not God. Nothing less because I want to be found obedient, God's daughter in whom He's well-pleased. The moment we set ourselves to seek God's will for our lives like this, we are heard on high (Daniel 10:12). And the more revelation is given, the more we obey the Father.

Like Daniel when the angel visited him to reveal war strategies, the revelation to pray third-heaven prayers is a war strategy for this season. Blood has been coursing down the streets of my very city, Charlotte, North Carolina, due to riotous protests over a black police officer shooting a black civilian. We are at war with the enemy of mankind, for we know he comes to kill, steal, and destroy all of humanity (John 10:10).

The Lord has been giving revelation to the saints for such a time as this. Like with Esther, the King of Kings has extended His scepter. In times of war, we must call a fast for the people of God as Esther did. God's solution, His preferred weapon of warfare, has always been prayer, fasting, and worshipping, not violence. When we pray and fast, the battle is the Lord's. When we worship, the enemies destroy themselves (2 Chronicles 20:20–22). When the Elisha's of today pray, their eyes are opened to see that there are many more of us than there are of the enemy (2 Kings 6:17)!

So it is in the time of battle that we don't care about being famous on Earth or in heaven. War purifies motives, allegiances, etc., knocking over the false gods in our lives. Battle ensues in the first heaven (Earth) and in the second heaven (unseen realm of Satan). The angel told Daniel that he battled the Prince of Persia for twenty-one days (second-heaven battle) until Michael helped him defeat the Prince of Persia so that the angel could get to Daniel to deliver a message. The angel then explained Daniel's vision that concerned the future of Daniel's people, the Israelites (Daniel 10:12–14).

The late Kim Clement's word from October 19, 2007, in Frederick, Maryland, has played out in the Trump administration:

"*What happened in the day of Daniel, he had a holy visitation from an angel because of fasting and praying. 'I will bring back that same hunger into My people. There will be manifestations of angels that shall come, and they shall bring forth the truth. The scrolls shall be opened, and [just like] the Prince of Persia struggled with the angel, because of that, there was a delay of twenty-one days. There has been a delay for a certain amount of time, but the Prince of Darkness of Persia has been struck down and destroyed' says the Spirit of God.*"

"*Hear these words before you even endeavor to take them in and eat the manna which I am giving you tonight.*

"*There is one more thing that took place with Daniel that will take place. I spoke to you about prayer, the ignition of prayer everywhere, not only in the prison but in the palace; not only in the dark house but in the White House. Prayer restored like the prayer of Daniel. Lions overcome because of the perception of Daniel. Middle Eastern kings, princes, sheiks calling on him behind the cloth. 'Yeshua, Yeshua,' shouting out from the youth in Iran, shouting out from the youth in Pakistan, shouting out from the youth of Israel. 'Yeshua' on the streets of Jerusalem. 'Yeshua' from Mt. Carmel. . . .*

"*Men stood alone in that day before the great battles that this nation has experienced. They stood, and they looked up to the one and only God. My Spirit yearns and longs for that day again when men will lay down arms, will lay down intelligence and lift up the sword of faith and declare the battle is not ours; it is the Lord's. This is where you're at now,' says the Lord. 'Rejoice, America, rejoice.'*"

Kim Clement's word above focused the body of Christ on the book of Daniel.

My friend, who gave me the scroll, declared to me that the end-times of Daniel are upon us. During the end-times, the remnant will be safe. We are not to fear. Those of us who are the remnant, our names will be written in the book [of God's plan for His own] (Daniel 12:1 Amplified version). This includes both Jew and Gentile and those who "sleep in the dust of the earth" who are raised to everlasting life" (John 5:29, Daniel 12:2). This book has been sealed until the time of the end (Daniel 12:4).

KIM CLEMENT—TRUMP PROPHECIES

The late Kim Clement also had powerful words of prophecy about Donald Trump. On April 4, 2007, Clement prophesied,

> *"Trump shall become a trumpet," says the Lord. "No, you didn't hear Me. Trump shall become a trumpet. Are you listening to Me? I will raise up the Trump to become a trumpet."*

Prior to this prophecy, on February 10, 2007, in Scottsdale, Arizona, Clement said,

> *"There will be a praying president, not a religious one. For I will fool the people," says the Lord. "I will fool the people. Yes, I will. The one that is chosen shall go in, and they shall say, 'He has hot blood.'"*
>
> *For the Spirit of God says, "Yes, he may have hot blood, but he will bring the walls of protection on this country in a*

greater way, and the economy of this country shall change rapidly," says the Lord of Hosts.

Listen to the Word of The Lord.

The Lord says, "I will put at your helm for two terms, a president that will pray, but he will not be a praying president when he starts. I will put him in office, and I will baptize him with the Holy Spirit and My power," says the Lord of Hosts.

". . . There is a president who will come," and God says, "he will have absolutely no fear. Absolutely no fear. Will be decisive. Make decisions. And then in the middle of the restoration of America rapidly because of a source of energy that shall come—quickly—and because miracle breakthroughs that shall come and because of agreements between nations, specifically China."

God said, "They never dreamed this would happen. When they shall say, 'Christ will reign, and we shall not implement—at all—socialism.' When they have said, 'We will make history without God.' No, you will not. No, you will not," says the Lord.

"For they are saying, 'How do we kill the giant? How do we kill the giant of debt? How do we kill the giant of socialism? How do we kill the giant of human secularism?'

"I have placed that man among you." . . . And God says, "These that shall reject him shall be shocked at how he takes the giant down.

"And they shall say, 'What is your plan for this, this giant?'

"And he shall take a simple stone. . . . And he will hold it up, *and they will laugh at him. But the plan is so brilliant," says the Lord. "It could only have been given by Me.*

"They will shout, 'IMPEACH! IMPEACH!' But this shall not happen." And then God says, "Highly embarrassing moments when another Snowden arises. And people will become very afraid. . . ."[3]

Amos 3:7 says, "Surely the Sovereign LORD does nothing without revealing his plan to his servants the prophets." Clearly, God revealed His plans for America through Prophet Kim Clement who passed away before Trump took office.

PROPHECY AT THE ROUNDTABLE WITH TRUMP

I mentioned earlier that I had the honor of sitting at the Clergy Roundtable a couple of seats away from Donald Trump on October 14, 2016. At that roundtable, Pastor Jorge Parrott spoke boldly and prophetically to Trump.

Parrott said, ". . . I believe the Lord is calling you into this great transformation of your life, but this is what you were created for. . . . The opportunity is there for you to become known as . . . one of the new Fathers of this great nation. . . . I saw the other day that after you are elected president, you will have an opportunity to sign a treaty with Israel, which will get a lot of resistance from all around the world, but it's gonna go through, and it's gonna be a tremendous spiritual and financial blessing to America and to Israel."

Well, as we all know, Trump was elected as Jorge foresaw. On May 14, 2018, President Trump officially relocated the U.S. Embassy in Israel from Tel Aviv to Jerusalem, recognizing Jerusalem as the capital of Israel.

On August 13, 2020, President Trump, Prime Minister Benjamin Netanyahu of Israel, and Sheikh Mohammed Bin Zayed (Crown Prince of Abu Dhabi and Deputy Supreme Commander of the United Arab Emirates) announced the historic peace treaty that Jorge Parrott prophesied to Trump about in that 2016 Clergy Roundtable that I attended.

How can anyone say that God Almighty was not using Donald Trump to bring peace to this world? In my opinion, Trump *is* one of the new Fathers of America!

MY INTERVIEW WITH JOY LAMB BEFORE THE 2016 ELECTION

God also spoke to a dear friend of mine, Joy Lamb, whom I taped before the 2016 presidential election. Joy is an amazing woman of God, a seasoned prayer warrior, and an excellent author on prayer. Please order her book, *The Sword of the Spirit*, a wonderful book on praying for our nation by going to TheSwordOfTheSpiritBook.com.

On two different occasions, while in prayer, the Lord instructed Joy to write Donald Trump notes, telling him to prepare to become president of the United States. Joy obeyed. In February 2011, five years before Trump announced his run for the presidency in 2016, Joy gave these notes to Trump's bellman at Trump Towers in New York, and later, to an associate at Mar-a-Lago where she and her husband were vacationing.

I posted my Interview with Joy Lamb on October 19, 2016

before the November 2016 election. You can watch the interview "Donica Interviews Joy Lamb" by visiting my website video page at DonicaHudson.com.[4]

God was preparing me by interviewing Joy—preparing me to understand that He is integrally involved in our election process, that He indeed had chosen a man to serve as the U.S. President, and that He is hearing our prayers to save America.

Joy also travelled with me on the Women for Trump bus tour that my good friend Nancy Schulze put together in 2016 for the Congressional Wives Speakers. I was honored to be a speaker in that group of powerful women.

Interviewing Joy Lamb who prophesied in 2011 about Trump's election

CELEBRATING THE LIFE OF
PETER "PETE" NORMAN
MARCH 14, 1940 – OCTOBER 3, 2016

SAINT PETE (NORMAN)

On October 3, 2016, a month before the 2016 presidential election, my media partner Sheila Cogan and I went to pray for one of my ministry prayer board members, Peter Norman. He had been ill, and we wanted to pray for his healing. My heart sank as I laid eyes on Pete who seemed emaciated, yet his crystal blue eyes were as bright as ever.

What happened next was seared in my mind.

Pete began to convey that he was seeing into heaven. He described the apostles, and then he began to tell us, "No worries . . . Trump is going to win."

Shocked, I explained gently to Pete that we didn't come to talk about politics—that we were there to pray for him. But he was having none of it. Heaven was already rejoicing that God had picked Trump to lead America, and he wanted us to know it!

Pete had served in the Navy and was a strong patriot, Christian father, grandfather, and husband to his wife Riley. His daughter Donna had been a friend for a long time and was there when Sheila and I visited.

We didn't know that when we left that day, Pete would graduate into heaven just four hours later.

I got choked up as I wrote this because God used such a precious man to speak to me in such a powerful way. I miss him. I am thankful to God for knowing Pete Norman and for allowing me to have a glimpse into heaven's realm there at Pete's bedside in the last few hours of his life on this earth.

I had the honor of ministering at Pete's graveside service. The regal military officers were there to honor Pete's service to our country. He served America and loved her with his final breaths.

CHOSEN

So, when people tell me that Donald Trump is horrible—and regurgitate vomitous mainstream media lies about him—I just smile. I know that God will vindicate Trump because God raised him up to slay the giants of socialism, the deep-state child-trafficking ring, poverty, and the cabal. Like King David, Trump is not perfect, but he was CHOSEN.

> LIKE KING DAVID, TRUMP IS NOT PERFECT, BUT HE'S CHOSEN.

So let's pray for him!

God's eye is roaming the earth looking for those who will serve Him (2 Chronicles 16:9)—grandmothers, grandfathers, mothers, fathers, children, teens—God is looking for those who will say, "Yes!"

Say, "Yes!"

PRAYER FOR FORMER PRESIDENT TRUMP AND FUTURE U.S. PRESIDENTS

Dear Lord,

We thank You that Your Word tells us that the heart of the king is in Your hand and that You turn it whichever way You desire. Therefore, we trust that the heart of our president is in Your hand and that You are directing his heart. May he always fear You, Lord, which is the beginning of wisdom so that he leads our nation during these difficult times with discernment and the ability to clearly distinguish between right and wrong. May our president find the same wisdom Abraham Lincoln found when "driven upon his knees many times by the overwhelming conviction that he had nowhere else to go" because his own wisdom "seemed inefficient for that day."[5]

We thank You for our president. We thank You that he has answered YOUR call to run for office, and You have kept him and his family safe. Please continue to cover him and his family and protect them from all evil. Surround our president with men and women who are loyal, trustworthy, and who do what is right in Your sight, Lord. May they always receive and offer godly counsel and live lives of integrity. We pray for our president and all of those in authority over us that we may lead quiet and peaceful lives in all godliness and honesty.

Lord, we know that Your Word tells us that You will bless those who bless Israel and curse those who curse Israel. We thank You that we had a president who blessed Israel! Thank You that President Trump moved the U.S. Embassy back to Jerusalem, recognizing Jerusalem as Israel's capital and reached a peace treaty with Israel and the UAE! Your Word tells us to pray for the peace of Jerusalem. Thank You, Lord, for using our former U.S. President to help bring peace to Jerusalem and to the Middle East. Lord, cause all future U.S. Presidents to bring peace as well.

Thank You for using President Trump to protect religious liberty in America. Call all future U.S. Presidents to preserve religious liberty for Americans. Restore us to our "first love" as a land which is one nation under God, indivisible, with liberty and justice for all.

Bring us godly U.S. Presidents who are bold, courageous, unhindered, and fearless in the face of global and national evil. Divinely protect them against all attempts to destroy their lives and the life of this nation.

Lord, we have heard the shocking public calls of the wicked to practice witchcraft against former President Trump. In the name of Jesus, we break and prevent every curse, hex, vex, or spell from alighting on President Trump, his family, and his former administration and upon any future U.S. Presidents. We thank You that You have given us authority over all powers of evil, and we declare that nothing shall by any means hurt our president and his family. We declare a bloodline of protection around Trump and all future U.S. Presidents. We pray that only the upright shall work in our government and that the wicked shall be exposed, cut off, and uprooted from our government. We declare an end to the deep state and the darkness that has sought to destroy our nation.

We declare that the spirit of mind control perpetrated by media lies, chaos, confusion, hatred, bitterness, lawlessness, and witchcraft will be broken in Jesus's mighty name. We declare that the scales will fall from the eyes of Americans as judgment is exacted upon those who have practiced evil in this country.

Vindicate the children, Lord. Punish those who have abused

Your little ones and enslaved women and children in human trafficking and sexual and satanic ritual abuse. Expose at every level—nationally and globally—those who have practiced the occult against women and children. Use our president to bring justice to our land.

Satan, you are a defeated foe. You will not ensnare this country and those within it any longer. We declare that the national sin of abortion shall be overturned as the hearts of the fathers are turned toward the children and the children to the fathers.

God, we thank You for giving former President Trump swift success in appointing pro-life Supreme Court Justices and lower court justices across America so that we may see abortion abolished as Roe v. Wade is overturned. We ask that You would convict all future U.S. Presidents to do the same in Jesus's name.

Lord, we pray for an end to all shedding of innocent blood, including abortion and all forms of child sacrifice. We humble ourselves, seek Your face, and pray that You would hear our prayers from heaven, forgive our sin, and heal our land.

In Jesus's name we pray, amen.

Scripture References to above prayer:

Romans 8:37	Proverbs 2:10–12,21,22
Proverbs 21:1	Psalm 33:12; 9:9
Deuteronomy 28:10,11	Acts 12:24
1 Timothy 2:1–3	

DECLARATIONS

We declare that You will restore America's ancient foundations so that America will once again be known as a city on the hill—a guiding light to the rest of the world—that blessed nation whose God is the Lord (Psalm 33:12). We honor the forefathers and Founding Fathers and Founding Mothers of our land that we might be a nation and a people who live long on the earth.

We declare that we are a free people because of Jesus's shed blood, which cleanses us from all unrighteousness.

Further, we thank You for our forefathers and foremothers who fought to secure our independence and our constitutional rights, many of whom shed their blood for our freedom as a nation. We declare an end to all socialism, Sharia law, communism, and Marxism in America aimed at destroying our nation's covenant Constitution and enslaving America to dictatorship, globalism, and a one-world government.

We declare that Jesus is Lord over our president and over the United States of America. We put our voices in agreement with former President Trump when he declared, "IN AMERICA, WE DON'T WORSHIP GOVERNMENT. WE WORSHIP GOD!"[6]

Amen!

CHAPTER 7

THE HIDDEN PRAYER FORCE OF HEAVEN

F=MA

NATURALLY SPEAKING, *force* equals *mass* times *acceleration*. It's important to understand "force" both naturally and spiritually. We are pretty good at understanding force as a science formula. Are you gonna be more afraid of the force of a tiny pebble thrown at you or the force of a large rock thrown at you at the same speed and distance away?

The large rock because it's got more force!

Same principle in football. Who would you be more afraid to be tackled by, a 95-pound linebacker or a 225-pound linebacker hitting you at the same speed?

The 225-pounder because his mass times his acceleration would squash you!

Now, would you rather be accidentally hit in the head by a penny dropped from a closet shelf or by a penny dropped from the top of the Empire State Building?

If you understand acceleration, you'd better prefer the penny from the closet shelf because a penny dropped from the top of the Empire State Building could kill you due to the increased force from acceleration.

So it is in the spirit realm.

Spiritually speaking, there's a force of covenant and history that accelerates over time. The force of covenant increases as it gains mass through agreement (Joshua 23:10), accelerating over time in history. We find these covenants first in the Bible and throughout history in civil covenants made between God and man. As Christians, with dual citizenship in heaven and on Earth, we can agree in prayer with biblically based covenants that connect heaven and Earth in a sense, such as when a covenant between God and man is established on Earth, it is recognized in heaven, marshaling the forces of heaven on Earth to preserve that covenant. However, when that covenant is under siege—whether it's a marital covenant or a civil covenant like America's Constitution—there's a spiritual war that must be waged to preserve that covenant. Agreement has been lost and must be regained.

> SPIRITUALLY SPEAKING, THERE'S A FORCE OF COVENANT AND HISTORY THAT ACCELERATES OVER TIME.

What's God's solution?

Re-covenanting prayer!

When marital covenants have been under siege, the bride and groom often recommit themselves in marriage with a renewal of the vows ceremony—a "re-covenanting" ceremony.

When Israel had kings who usurped God's place, the Israelites were held accountable for it. Nehemiah 8–9 shows us how on multiple occasions, the Israelites "re-covenanted" with God by repentance of sins and a reaffirmation of the covenant.

So it is with America. The enemy of the state—the enemy of our souls—has been long at work duping Americans into believing that we are not a Christian nation.

We are!

. . . that we do not have a *covenant* Constitution blessed by God and literally *forged in a holy tripartite image—a truth the enemy hopes you never discover!*

We do! (More on that later.)

. . . that we should replace our democratic form of government with socialism, communism, or Marxism.

We should *not*!

With socialism, communism, and Marxism, government is god! Our Founding Fathers believed that only God was sovereign when creating our Constitution. They sought to keep the government out of the Church, *not* the Church out of the government. *We the people* who are the Church need to occupy government offices, serve our country with sacrificial love, and stop the government from stealing our religious liberties. Socialism, communism, and Marxism strip countries of any form of religion.

WITH SOCIALISM, COMMUNISM, AND MARXISM, GOVERNMENT IS GOD!

Most westernized Christians have been tricked into believing that civil government has nothing to do with our faith. They've bought the lie of separation of Church and State (which is never mentioned in our founding documents). Many Christians are like frogs in the hot pot that's about to boil, and we don't even realize it.

Our Founding Fathers certainly did not believe this. In fact, they were very familiar with "re-covenanting."

Everything God established in the Bible was through covenant. God covenanted with night and day when creating our universe. He covenanted with Abraham when setting the stage to bring the Messiah into humanity. He announced Himself as the God of Abraham, Isaac, and Jacob, which pointed to covenant.

JACOB'S LADDER CONNECTING HEAVEN AND EARTH

In Genesis 28:10–22, Jacob is visited by the Lord in a dream where angels are ascending and descending on a ladder connecting Earth to heaven. The Lord echoes the covenant promises He made with Jacob's forefathers, Isaac and Abraham.

> *He stands beside Jacob and says, "I am the Lord, the God of Abraham thy Father, and the God of Isaac. The land where on thou liest, to thee will I give it, and to thy seed. And thy seed shall be as the dust of the earth and thou shalt spread abroad to the west, and to the east, and to the north, and to the south. And in thee and in thy seed shall all the families of the earth be blessed (Genesis 28:13–14).*

The Lord's quoting of the Abrahamic covenant indicates that this covenant is also recognized in heaven. It's important to realize that Jacob was in Abraham (covenant explained in Chapter 5), and Jacob also receives the covenant promise made to his grandfather Abraham.

Did you know that generational blessings that your forefathers or foremothers may have petitioned God for can manifest in your life because you are "in them" through the bloodline? In the same way, as citizens of the United States, we are joined in civil covenant with our founding fathers of faith. We are "in them" through civil covenant and the blood covenant in Christ and have a jurisdictional authority to pray third-heaven prayers.

Jacob's ladder connecting heaven and Earth lends credence to the Lord's prayer where Jesus instructs us to pray, "Let it be done on earth as it is in heaven." This is a great example of a third-heaven prayer!

The "angels ascending and descending" in Jacob's dream is the same language Jesus uses in John 1:51: "And he saith unto him, Verily, verily, I say unto you, Hereafter ye shall see heaven open, and the angels of God ascending and descending upon the Son of man."

Early nineteenth-century Methodist theologian Adam Clarke explains that "angels ascending and descending upon the Son of Man, is a metaphor taken from the custom of dispatching couriers or messengers from the prince to his ambassador in a foreign court and from the ambassador back to the prince."[1]

Jesus's shed blood truly provides the covenant bridge to heaven for all of us who have covenanted with Him as Lord and Savior. As a result, we now have dual citizenship on Earth and in heaven, replete with our own ambassador angels who ascend and descend as we join what I call the "prayer force of heaven."

TWO KEYS TO UNLOCKING THE PRAYER FORCE OF HEAVEN ON EARTH

Two keys are available to us if we want to unlock the prayer force of heaven here on Earth to save America:

1. Prayer agreement with civil covenants recognized in heaven
2. Prayer agreement between Church and State authorities here on Earth

KEY #1 PRAYER AGREEMENT WITH CIVIL COVENANTS RECOGNIZED IN HEAVEN

The first key is agreeing with the covenantal aspects of the Founding Father's civil covenants, such as the Constitutions of our nation and our fifty states, that are recognized in heaven. It invokes God's protection over our country and marshals heaven's hidden angelic forces to preserve our covenant roots and religious liberties. This type of prayer often can be done on a local level with your own town or city covenants that invoke God's name.

A good example of re-covenanting on a local level was in my own city of Charlotte. The North Carolina Legislative Prayer Caucus, of which I was a member, prayed with city leaders and re-covenanted to preserve our religious liberty on the 240th anniversary of the

Mecklenburg Declaration of Independence. We had the authority of Church and State agreeing in prayer to Almighty God—the same God Charlotte's Founding Fathers had appealed to when penning the Declaration.

Does your city have a root of religious freedom? Have you found the clause in your state's Constitution invoking divine interposition that you can re-covenant with? I share the prayer that I've done with my City of Charlotte as a guide for others in the next section.

CHARLOTTE'S ROOT OF RELIGIOUS FREEDOM

Christians have an advantage when it comes to political activism. The indwelling Holy Spirit coupled with the biblical Holy Scriptures can guide us into understanding spiritual roots including political ones. This gives us insight and understanding for advocating for legislation to be established that reflects God's will on Earth for mankind. When the bathroom bill catapulted Charlotte to Jerusalem-like global media coverage, I knew that "the enemy was trying to put the axe to the root" (Matthew 3:10) of Charlotte's religious freedom covenant and our nation's original religious freedom covenant. The Mecklenburg Declaration of Independence was signed May 20, 1775 by Presbyterian elders and a pastor who declared themselves in Resolve 3 to be:

> *"free and independent people [who] are, and of right ought to be, a sovereign and self-governing Association, under the control of no power other than that of our God and the General Government of the Congress; to the maintenance of*

which independence, we solemnly pledge to each other, our mutual co-operation, our lives, our fortunes and our most sacred honor."[2]

This is the covenantal clause we prayed through when asking the Lord once again to intervene and to preserve our religious liberty in Charlotte. Thankfully, He did!

Interestingly enough, the idea of civil re-covenanting is not new. I was surprised to find that Reverend Alexander Craighead, a Founding Father of Mecklenburg County who pastored seven area churches in the 1700s, wrote pamphlets on renewal of covenants where breaches needed restoring.

"In 1742, Rev. Craighead published a pamphlet in which he set forth his views on civil government, and the Christian's duty towards a Covenant-breaking nation."[3] Craighead believed that the Church, as well as the nation, should renew the covenants. He wrote "the first treatise published in America to denounce the monarch of Great Britain a tyrant (King Charles II) . . . the 1743 Renewal of the Scottish National Covenant and Solemn League and Covenant."[4]

And guess who published it, along with two other works of Craighead's?

Benjamin Franklin. Remember, Bonnie Chavda's encounter in the Charlotte area began with Benjamin Franklin's last living relative. Bonnie continues to work alongside the other pastors of Charlotte to restore Mecklenburg County to its covenantal roots.

God is on His way again, tracing the ancient routes of salvation (Habakkuk 3:3).

A SPIRITUAL JERUSALEM

You see, Charlotte is a *key* city to capture if you're an enemy of America. If you want to kill a nation, you put the axe to the root of the original covenants. Believe it or not, Charlotte's Mecklenburg Declaration of Independence is one of those first covenants for religious liberty. I believe that's why Charlotte has convulsed with so much violence, turmoil, and murder with riots, HB2, and the RNC being shut down. It's much like when a person gets delivered from a stronghold, he or she must be filled with the Holy Spirit or the enemy will return with the "friends and family plan" of seven spirits worse to occupy its former habitation.[5]

IF YOU WANT TO KILL A NATION, YOU PUT THE AXE TO THE ROOT OF THE ORIGINAL COVENANTS.

The Church in Charlotte must rise up, deliver her city, occupy the land, and reform its laws to sustain God's presence and power. That's why I have fought so hard in the public square and on my knees to protect my children from unbelievable false educational indoctrinations like the push to open up Charlotte's bathrooms, locker rooms, and showers to members of the opposite biological sex and the "Gender Unicorn," which was created by a national transgender youth group and used to train all Charlotte Mecklenburg School principals.

As local Pastor Rick Joyner states in Larry Sparks's book *Prophetic Words for 2020*, "To say that God gave somebody the body of one gender but the heart of the opposite gender is an affront to God. It implies that He did not know what He was doing but made such mistakes when He made us. This begins to erode our faith in him in everything else. Men and women who are in confusion about who they are will not be able to become who they were created to be unless the confusion is cleared up."[6]

God is raising up voices of clarity and compassion in America and in Charlotte, North Carolina. If you have struggled with gender confusion and identity issues, Jesus can set you free. See prayer at end of this chapter.

I call Charlotte a "spiritual Jerusalem" where God is drawing the Messianic and the Gentile remnant (Isaiah 10:21) for an end-time outpouring of God's Spirit—i.e. revival! God uses biblical patterns in our current day (Habakkuk 3:3). I've prayed for revival in Charlotte for almost thirty years now.

Donica with Former Charlotte Mayor and Congresswoman Sue Myrick

As a result, I always asked my guests on my TV show *Charlotte Alive*, "What brought you to Charlotte?" because I wanted to know if their answers involved revival. As a result, my shows ended up being replete with awe-inspiring stories of God leading people to Charlotte for the purpose of revival.

One of my favorite shows is an interview I did with revivalist Henry Blackaby, respected pastor and best-selling author of *Experiencing God*. (You can find his video interview "Henry Blackaby on Charlotte Alive" on my website DonicaHudson.com)[7] Blackaby told me that he knew Charlotte was destined for revival when he prayed with former Charlotte Mayor Sue Myrick from her office overlooking the City of Charlotte. He recalled how Myrick prayed with tears for our city. Myrick went on to serve as Congresswoman for North Carolina.

MESSIANIC AND GENTILE REMNANTS

To me, it was a monumental sign that Charlotte is much closer to revival when Billy Graham Evangelical Association headquarters moved to Billy Graham's hometown of Charlotte. Revivalist Dr. Michael Brown (*FIRE School of Ministry*, *Ask Dr. Brown*, and *The Line of Fire* shows) had already moved to the Charlotte area out of the Brownsville Revival in Florida. Then Sid Roth moved his ministry Messianic Vision and television show *It's Supernatural!* here where other Messianic media ministers like my friends, David and Barbara Cerullo (Inspiration Networks), are established. Basically, Charlotte is the root of evangelism (Billy Graham), root of Christian media (Jim Bakker's PTL, Cerullo's INSP, Sid Roth's and Dr. Brown's media, to name a few), and a root of religious freedom (Mecklenburg Declaration of Independence 1775). A three-stranded cord is not easily broken, but the enemy has tried.

THE REMNANT REVIVES THE ROOT

The "Meck Deck," fondly termed by Charlotteans, was signed a year before our national Declaration of Independence in Philadelphia on July 4, 1776. The "Meck Deck" is a civil covenant, which makes Charlotte a covenant city just like Jerusalem. *We the people,* who are the Judeo-Christian Church, are the remnant charged with reviving that root, spiritually speaking.

A pro-life conservative and orthodox Jew, Ben Shapiro, stated to Catholic business executives at a 2019 Legatus Conference, "The future of the United States . . . will depend on, 'an alliance of all people who believe in Judeo-Christian values and the God who created them. . . .'"[8]

Shapiro was pointing to the Enlightenment resultant from thousands of years of a belief system stemming from the Ten Commandments and the Sermon on the Mount creating the modern world. "There is an entire contingent of Americans who want to destroy the roots of their own civilization. . . . Because you [Catholics] represent the roots of civilization, and I believe that my religion represents the roots of civilization: to destroy the roots of civilization means that the tree will wither and die."[9]

THE SIN OF SLAVERY

The fact that our nation's civil covenants are recognized in heaven as they are on Earth does not make them devoid of sin. Slavery is and was evil. It was never God's will for America. His perfect will was for America to be a land where all men are created equal, not enslaved.

So why would anyone want to pray a re-covenanting prayer over our nation's Constitution when slavery was originally permitted and practiced by some of the Founding Fathers?

For one, slavery was abolished! When praying a re-covenanting prayer, we re-covenant with the portion of the document that calls upon God and invokes His blessing, i.e. His divine guidance or protection—or in the case of the Constitution, His protection of our religious liberty and our democratic republic. We are not agreeing with a practice that was evil and then was later abolished.

American abolitionist and former slave Frederick Douglass said in his famed "What is the Fourth of July to the Slave?" speech on July 5, 1852, that "the Declaration of Independence is the ringbolt to the chain of your nation's destiny." Although the man who wrote the Declaration of Independence owned slaves, Douglass contended that Thomas Jefferson's philosophy and the "genius of American institutions"—the constitutional system built by the Founding Fathers—would lead to the destruction of slavery.

Douglass was right.

But what has Marxism wrought?

The words and philosophy of Jefferson and America's other Founding Fathers made free men out of slaves. The communist ideology of Marx and Engels made slaves out of free men and plunged large parts of the globe into misery, tyranny, and darkness.

If one wants liberty and justice—and racial equality—for all, we are far better served looking to Jefferson, Douglass, and Abraham Lincoln than the failed doctrines of Marx and Engels.[10]

Black Lives Matter (BLM) organization founder Patrisse Khan-Cullors proudly stated in a 2015 interview with Real News Network that she and her cofounders were "trained Marxists."[11] Since the heinous death of George Floyd at the hands of police brutality, BLM has surged with millions of dollars in funding, all with the covert point of destroying our nation's Constitution and replacing it with Marxism.

Interestingly for you Christian readers, BLM also supports

the rise of a one-world government and the destruction of the nuclear family.

I think we all can agree that as followers of Christ, the statement, "black lives matter" is absolutely true. But the Marxist Black Lives Matter organization will kill our nation.

Americans should not just study our U.S. Constitution because people want to take away our freedom, but we should study our Constitution so that we know our rights and can defend them. Furthermore, when you learn about the origin of the Constitution and our Founding Fathers, you can see God's truth woven all through it!

What do I mean?

When our Founding Fathers were hammering out the U.S. Constitution, they kept in mind two foundational principles, truths that will stand the test of time: 1. Man is sinful. 2. Only God is sovereign. This was how former slave and abolitionist Frederick Douglass voiced faith as quoted above in a "constitutional system built by the Founding Fathers [that] would lead to the destruction of slavery."

Douglass had faith in the constitutional system because it was built upon timeless principles of truth from the Bible. Moreover, "It is squarely based upon the federalist tradition of covenantal theology."[12]

The constitutional system of checks and balances is designed to prevent any form of absolute sovereignty so that *we the people* maintain control of the republic, thereby limiting big government.

TRUTH THE ENEMY HOPES YOU NEVER DISCOVER
In fact, the three branches of America's government crafted in our nation's Constitution reflect our three-partite God.

For the Lord is our Judge, the Lord is our law giver, the Lord is our King; He will save us (Isaiah 33:22).

Founding Father James Madison was responsible for the three-part government of the United States (judicial, legislative, and executive) inspired by Isaiah 33:22. Cancel culture has tried and succeeded for the most part in making Americans believe that we do not have a Christian heritage with foundational documents inspired by God's Word.

WASHINGTON AND LINCOLN

Two founding fathers who grew to believe slavery was wrong were George Washington and Abraham Lincoln. Though a slave owner, Washington began questioning slavery during the Revolutionary War, when he led the North American colonies' battle for independence from Great Britain.[13]

Washington states in 1786, "*I never mean (unless some particular circumstance should compel me to it) to possess another slave by purchase: it being among my first wishes to see some plan adopted by the legislature by which slavery in the Country may be abolished by slow, sure, & imperceptible degrees.*"[14]

When he drafted his will at age 67, George Washington included a provision that would free the 123 enslaved people he owned outright. This bold decision marked the culmination of two decades of introspection and inner conflict for Washington, as his views on slavery changed gradually but dramatically.[15]

Washington also states in 1786 that "*There is not a man living who wishes more sincerely than I do, to see a plan adopted for this abolition of [slavery] but there is only one proper and effectual mode by which it can be accomplished, & that is by Legislative authority.*"[16]

Equally disturbed by the evil of slavery, Abraham Lincoln ran for president in 1860 on an antislavery platform as a Republican. This "made him extremely unpopular with Southerners and his nomination for President in 1860 enraged them. On November 6, 1860, Lincoln won the presidential election without the support of a single Southern state. Talk of secession, bandied about since the 1830s, took on a serious new tone. The Civil War was not entirely caused by Lincoln's election, but the election was one of the primary reasons the war broke out the following year."[17]

While the Civil War raged. Lincoln called upon the prayer force of heaven by issuing a "Proclamation for a Day of Prayer, Fasting, and Humiliation" March 30, 1863.[18] After this day of seeking the Lord, the North won, and slavery was abolished. To learn more about this, visit DonicaHudson.com and view my "Invitation of Honor" which was sent to all fifty United States governors imploring them to issue prayer proclamations for their states modeled after Lincoln's prayer proclamation.[19]

MYSTERY TO THE ANCIENT GATES OF JUSTICE IN THE SOUTH—AN APPEAL TO HEAVEN TO HEAL THE LAND (HEBREWS 11:39-40)

Many times, as we follow the Holy Spirit, He will lead us into amazing, life-changing adventures that will forever shape our identity. My experiences with Pastor Andre Vaynol from South Africa have been like this.

I first met Pastor Andre when I was asked to do a TV interview with him during the severe 2007 drought in North Carolina. Pastor Andre had been given a dream and a word about Native American reconciliation needed from America's sin of the Trail of Tears. The evidence of this "national sin" was a drought that was plaguing the North Carolina region.

God tapped me to tape him. That interview began a strong relationship that continues to this day. To see the interview and what God did through Pastor Andre's obedience, visit DonicaHudson. com and view the video "Breaking the North Carolina Drought" from my Native American Reconciliation video series[20] By the way, I ended up being asked to mail DVDs of this interview to the White House and to the North Carolina governor's office after former founding CEO of New Dominion Bank Bradley Thompson took Andre to both places to share his word.

Now, South Africa, where Andre lives, has enough of its own problems. I took notice when God sent a man halfway around the world to speak to our region about a Trail of Tears that he knew nothing about historically when he first dreamed about it.

This shows us that God can tap any of us. What has He shown you? We just have to be available and willing to go. "Here I am, Lord, send me!" (Isaiah 6:8).

Andre's interview kicked off a series of other great interviews that exposed a major breach in the ancient foundations of our country. As Andre had admonished in his interview, America had to repent for the treaties with Native Americans that our government broke which led to the Trail of Tears. See my interview with Negiel Bigpond "Removing the Curse from the Land" on the Native American Reconciliation Series playlist to learn more about the broken treaties.[21]

To repair this exposed breach, God tapped Alison Muesing to plan a "Day of Remembrance Ceremony" on May 30, 2008 in

Murphy, North Carolina. Off I went to videotape this ceremony. I was eight months huge in pregnancy with my third child, Lucas, and sweating bullets in the heat of the drought on that mountain in Murphy. It felt like it was 110 degrees. Tony and Lee Mazzone held umbrellas in the sun because it felt like we were all getting sunburnt as we drew up like raisins. Nevertheless, God moved.

This ceremony was a monumental event which brought U.S. governmental authority together with Indian tribal authority as government leaders repented for breaking treaties with Native Americans. As a result, the drought that had lingered for over a year, bankrupting businesses and costing millions, was finally broken. We even experienced light rain at that mountain after the ceremony concluded.

I had the honor of interviewing some wonderful leaders who answered God's call to participate in this ceremony, including Congressman Zach Wamp from Chattanooga, Tennessee, cosponsor of the Resolution of Apology for Native American People and who now helps to lead the National Prayer Breakfast in Washington; Greg Richardson, Executive Director of North Carolina Commission of Indian Affairs; Senator Snow from Western North Carolina; Native American Pastor Clifton Pettit of Marble City, Oklahoma; and John Partin, whose family descended from Cherokee Chief John Ross, Cherokee leader on the Trail of Tears in 1838. You can view all of these interviews on my website DonicaHudson.com.[22]

This was my first foray into understanding how to become a "repairer of the breach." Those "Ancient Gates of Justice in the South" that Negiel Bigpond addressed swung wide open as the King of Glory came in to bring healing to the land.

And your ancient ruins shall be rebuilt; you shall raise up the foundations of many generations; you shall be called the repairer of the breach. . . . (Isaiah 58:12 ESV).

Lift up your heads, O ye gates; even lift them up, ye everlasting doors; and the king of glory shall come in (Psalm 24:7 KJV).

Interviewing Congressman Zach Wamp at DAY OF REMEMBRANCE CEREMONY, June 2008

ANOTHER BREACH EXPOSED

In May 2013, I interviewed Pastor Andre again. He revealed that America was under judgment. He proposed that the solution to this judgement is rooted in a historical example, Abraham Lincoln's Proclamation for a Day of Prayer, Fasting and Humiliation, which brought an end to the Civil War and abolished slavery. During that radio interview, Vaynol made a call for someone to draft a prayer proclamation like Lincoln's to bring healing to the land.

Not eager for another assignment that required intensive work, I hoped someone listening to the radio would pick up that baton and run with it. Six months passed, and the Lord made it clear that I was to draft a modern-day prayer proclamation and ask Governor McCrory to sign it. It took another year and a half before I was able to get the proclamation crafted and signed!

When I awoke on Memorial Day morning in 2015, the Lord said, "I've applied the blood to North Carolina. Get up. You're safe." I knew what the Lord was referring to—North Carolina was safe from judgment. In His omniscience, God foresaw how the Prayer Proclamation would be used to summon the prayer force of heaven to stop the violence and bloodshed during the 2016 Charlotte Riots.

Later that day, I received a call from my assistant stating that the governor had signed the Proclamation.

For many months, I didn't know the date to put on the Proclamation. The Lord finally revealed it to be the date of the original civil covenant for religious freedom in North Carolina—May 20, 1775. God allowed us to go to the very spot on Trade and Tryon streets where the Mecklenburg Declaration of Independence was signed and read the Proclamation aloud.

God further prepared the ground here in Charlotte by having Doug Stringer bring The Response to our city in September 2015. The Response USA was a call to prayer for a nation in crisis. Doug Stringer led The Response and only went to states by Gubernatorial invitation where state governors would attend and participate. He definitely understands the jurisdictional authority and protection that a state governor's prayer brings to the state.

I came to understand that the Proclamation was a pre-emptive strike on the Lord's part that we blindly carried out in obedience to His word through Pastor Andre—to preserve religious freedom through the civil covenant in the "Meck Deck."

God brought me to this understanding when my friend, Robert Whitlow, whom I revere greatly, watched Azusa Now and ordered an Appeal to Heaven flag. My friend then brought that flag to our small group and wrapped it upon my shoulders and prophesied over me. Now this kind of thing doesn't happen all the time. I could feel the gravity of the mantle of the assignment that was being confirmed.

Robert is an attorney, best-selling Christian author, and Christian movie producer. He obeys the Holy Spirit. He does not go around throwing Appeal to Heaven flags on people all the time. Because of his obedience, God began to reveal through Dutch Sheets's book *An Appeal to Heaven* the reasons why God had put a mandate on me and others in Charlotte to agree with our forefathers for religious freedom.

I believe Charlotte is the "Ancient Gate of Justice of the South" because we were the first county and state to declare religious freedom in America in 1775—a year before the nation's Declaration of Independence in 1776. God has since called me to proclaim this on multiple occasions from multiple platforms. Particularly memorable was the May 30, 2015 Rally at the Cross at the Billy Graham Library exactly seven years after the Day of Remembrance Repentance Ceremony on May 30, 2008, where North Carolina's drought was broken.

KEY #2 PRAYER AGREEMENT BETWEEN CHURCH AND STATE AUTHORITIES

In September 2016, Charlotte erupted in riots after the shooting death of Keith Lamont Scott. Watching the rioting, looting, and more murder on the news was horrifying. I wrote in my journal that "blood was coursing down the streets of my city."

That Wednesday night, we gathered for our prayer meeting and stood around the Appeal to Heaven flag asking God to stop the bloodshed. The next day, I was in communication with my good friends, Bishop Jackson and Pastor Threatt. Threatt asked me to join him and the rest of the black pastors of Charlotte at a prayer vigil in Romare Bearden Park, the heart of downtown Charlotte where another murder had occurred the previous night.

Threatt said, "And bring the Prayer Proclamation."

So my media partner, Sheila, and I lit out for downtown. We knew we were on a mission from God and that we would be safe. We prayed for a parking spot nearby. God blessed us with one. When we got there, the Billy Graham Rapid Response Team Chaplains greeted us.

My heart was filled with courage and gratitude as I watched these bold and courageous men of God—the black pastoral fathers of the city—calling for peace in the midst of racial rioting and bloodshed. They felt the pain of the community, and they were asserting their spiritual authority to bring healing and peace.

Pastor Threatt said, "I want you to speak last."

I gulped hard.

Here I was, the only woman slated to speak holding this large piece of paper that our governor had signed. No one else but Pastor

Threatt and Bishop Jackson really knew what that paper was. Pastor Threatt, a former Marine who possesses both mantles of Church and State, understood the significance of that Prayer Proclamation.

When it came time for me to step up to the microphone, I knew I had to "suck it up" and speak with authority. The mission was greater than me.

What happened next was the key that unlocked the prayer force of heaven on Earth that day.

God allowed me to read the signed Prayer Proclamation. As the pastoral authority of the Church agreed with the governmental authority of the State through that Prayer Proclamation, the forces of heaven were summoned. We echoed the prayers of Abraham Lincoln who saw slavery abolished after calling upon the Lord with his Proclamation for a Day of Prayer, Fasting, and Humiliation. As Dutch Sheets said in *An Appeal to Heaven*, we had "inserted ourselves in the timeline" and agreed with our forefather in the faith according to Hebrews 11:39–40.

That was when I realized the *force* we can have in prayer. There were no more deaths nor bloodshed! Thank you, Lord.

> WHAT HAPPENED NEXT WAS THE KEY THAT UNLOCKED THE PRAYER FORCE OF HEAVEN ON EARTH THAT DAY.

If our eyes had been opened to see the legions of angels that were mobilized to bring peace in Jesus's name, I'm sure we would've been in awe—like some sci-fi movie. Although we can't see the hidden force of heaven when we pray—much like we can't see the wind—we can see the *effects* of the prayer force—much like the wind.

There is power in agreement. "Again I say to you that if two of you agree on earth concerning anything that they ask, it will be done for them by My Father in heaven. For where two or three are gathered together in My name, I am there in the midst of them" (Matthew 18:19–20).

When we are praying in agreement with covenants that God has blessed, we can expect multiplied power as God's covenant people like the Israelites did in Deuteronomy 32:30 when battling. One had put a thousand to flight, and two had put ten thousand to flight. The Lord fought for them, and He will fight for us.

I don't believe there are formulas for faith. That really turns me off. Faith is a gift from God. The "formula" I'm about to offer is a mere mnemonic technique for illustrating the force of covenant and history that God impressed upon me. Those who are scientifically minded might appreciate this.

So if **F = MA** (**Force** equals **Mass** times **Acceleration**), scientifically as we discussed at the beginning of this chapter, then spiritually we could say that **F = CA** (**Force** of prayer equals **Covenant** times **Agreement**). Whether we are agreeing with the prayers of those Covenant saints who have gone before us or we are praying in agreement with their civil covenants, God honors those prayers.

If you remember Pastor Bonnie Chavda's vision from Chapter 6, the remnant of saints still on the earth must come into agreement with heaven. They have to begin sending up third-heaven prayers of agreement from Earth to dispel the yellow fog of chaos,

> F = CA (FORCE OF PRAYER EQUALS COVENANT TIMES AGREEMENT).

corruption, lies, bitterness, anger, rage, malice, witchcraft, and betrayal, to name a few, upon our nation.

Why do we need to do this?

Because when we agree with the prayers of our forefathers and founding covenantal documents like Abraham Lincoln's Prayer Proclamation or our nation's U.S. Constitution in prayer, we become restorers of the breach!

When we re-covenant in a renewal of the vows marriage ceremony, we strengthen the covenant.

When we re-covenant with our state's Constitution, we strengthen the covenant, and our hearts are strengthened to uphold it.

There's multiplied power in agreement, and the enemy knows it. That's why the current "cancel culture" is trying to cancel agreement in prayer by "cancelling the Founding Fathers" as evidenced by tearing down monuments all over America. If cancel culture can get Americans to believe that our Founders and our Constitution are bad, then there will be no agreement in prayer, and the breach in our country will remain—but the country may not.

> IF CANCEL CULTURE CAN GET AMERICANS TO BELIEVE THAT OUR FOUNDERS AND OUR CONSTITUTION ARE BAD, THEN THERE WILL BE NO AGREEMENT IN PRAYER AND THE BREACH IN OUR COUNTRY WILL REMAIN—BUT THE COUNTRY MAY NOT.

Those from among you will rebuild the ancient ruins; You will raise up the age-old foundations; And you will be called the repairer of the breach, The restorer of the streets in which to dwell (Isaiah 58:12).

America's covenants of the Constitution and the Declaration of Independence are most definitely breached. Most Americans don't even know the history of these covenants. They don't know the many godly men who signed them. Most Americans have never even read them entirely—including elected house members in Washington, as former Congressman Rick Green pointed out on video in the *Constitution Alive* series he hosts, which I highly recommend!

Clergy Prayer Vigil at Romare Beardon Park during 2016 Charlotte Riots— presenting and praying through Prayer Proclamation signed by Governor McCrory agreeing with Founding Father Abraham Lincoln's Prayer Proclamation of 1863.

Billy Graham Evangelistic Association Chaplain offers encouragement after speaking at Clergy Prayer Vigil during Charlotte Riots

PENNIES FROM HEAVEN

Therefore, since we are surrounded by such a great cloud of witnesses, let us throw off everything that hinders and the sin that so easily entangles, and let us run with perseverance the race marked out for us (Hebrews 12:1).

Sheila and I met a friend for lunch. Our friend was relaying a heavenly encounter that he'd had recently. I have never met anyone like this guy. He was humble, kind, and loved Jesus with his whole heart. He was telling us that as he'd slept the night before, he met Abraham Lincoln.

I could hardly believe my ears. "You what? Went to heaven? Met Abraham Lincoln?" I asked with great skepticism.

He said, "I don't really know. I just met him while I was sleeping."

I thought, *Must've been a dream.*

Then I remembered the words of the Apostle Paul: "I know a man in Christ who fourteen years ago was caught up to the third heaven. Whether it was in the body or out of it I do not know, but God knows" (2 Corinthians 12:2).

I quieted my mind and listened. He told us that the saints can hear us when we say their names. My mind raced to the Clergy Press Conference where I said Abraham Lincoln's name loudly in the middle of the Charlotte Riots in downtown in 2016. I had read the Proclamation for a Day of Prayer, Fasting, and Humiliation modelled after Lincoln's and praying his prayers!

I had studied a lot about Lincoln as I wrote the Prayer Proclamation. I loved that he was a godly man who hated slavery. I loved that he was a patriot who loved America and had the divine wisdom to call upon the Lord and see slavery abolished! So I was fascinated that our friend had met him in heaven. He couldn't tell me all that happened, but he did say that he was to encourage me—that Lincoln and the saints were praying for me.

Wait . . . *what?* "They *pray* in heaven?" I asked. "But I thought since you were in heaven, you no longer had to pray because you could speak directly to God."

My friend said, "They pray for those of us down here."

This was a concept I had never conceived of, but it made perfect sense.

But wait a minute—a person talking to Abraham Lincoln in his heavenly dreams?

Whether this was real or not, I wasn't sure—until Sheila came back from the restroom holding a shiny new penny in her palm—heads up—*Lincoln's* head. She was stunned because the penny had appeared at her feet. "The restroom had white floors," she said, "and this penny was not there at first. Then when I looked down again, it was at my feet."

This was my first experience with "pennies from heaven."

In the next couple of years that followed, my journal began to fill with pennies from heaven—all signs that God has been pointing us toward the preservation of America.

My friends Mollie, Kathy, and Bonnie had been receiving pennies too, not just old gummy pennies in dirt, but shiny ones in conspicuous places. We knew that God was trying to tell us something, but we weren't sure what. We got together and prayed.

Then, perhaps my biggest clue came when my broadcast partner Jim Quick and I went to Washington, DC to cover the March for Life in 2019. We wanted to be "boots on the ground" for folks who could not go to Washington in person to join the March to save the lives of the unborn. We livestreamed the March and got some really good interviews. My favorite was Jim Daly, President of Focus on the Family. (My interview with him titled "Donica interviews Jim Daly, Pres. FOCUS ON THE FAMILY" can be found on my website DonicaHudson.com.[23]) His story was so inspiring. We packed up our camera gear and headed back to our rendezvous point at a church parking lot in Virginia where Jim could get his car.

I'll never forget it . . . Jim's car was the only car in the vast parking lot. As he walked up to his car door, he bent down and looked up at me with incredulity and extended his hand toward me.

"You're never gonna believe this. It's a penny with the year of Roe v. Wade!"

THE NATIONAL OFFENSE

I was stunned when Jim presented that penny to me. I don't know about you, but I don't find 1973 pennies often, especially at my car door in a church parking lot when returning from a March for Life rally fighting abortion in our nation's capital! This was an undeniable sign from heaven that we were on the right track.

But it wasn't until I heard Dutch Sheets speak on the "offense" that had stopped the signs and wonders movement in America that I got the whole picture here.[24]

What was the national offense?

You got it—abortion.

Interviewing FOCUS ON THE FAMILY President Jim Daly at March For Life in Washington, D.C. Jan. 2019

Donica Hudson at March For Life in Washington DC January 2019

Jim Quick at March For Life in Washington DC January 2019

2019 March for Life

Family Research Council headquarters in Washington DC during March For Life 2019

*There are six things that the Lord hates, seven that are an abomination to him: haughty eyes, a lying tongue, and **hands that shed innocent blood** ... (Proverbs 6:16–19).*

The slaughtering of over 60 million babies now annually is an abomination that grieves our Creator enough that He withdrew those healings, miracles, signs, and wonders that Dutch describes were flowing in the '70s.[25]

What Dutch calls the "synergy of the ages," I call the "force of covenant and history."

Abortion was the breach in our covenant with God that has held up revival. And I'm afraid that it's opened wide the doors in the spirit realm for increased human trafficking and ritual abuse right under our noses here in America. If that breach is not repaired, I am afraid that our nation will suffer judgment so severe that we may never recover.

President Trump was fully committed to overturning Roe v. Wade. He gave a heartfelt speech to the faith community at the National Prayer Breakfast at Washington DC in February 2019. Jim Quick, Mollie Faison, and I attended that event as well. While there, I had the opportunity to interview Tony Perkins, President of the Family Research Council. This organization is a champion of pro-life policy.

ENTER DONALD J. TRUMP

Most Christians don't have eyes to see that God has taken a man who was a maverick, an entrepreneur, and a *fearless* wrecking ball to

political correctness and raised him up to absolutely abolish this abomination called abortion along with many other abominations, such as child trafficking.

But no presidential administration can do this without the Church. We must pray for God to intervene, and I believe we will see Roe v. Wade overturned!

Jim Quick & Mollie Faison at National Prayer Breakfast February 2019

NC Conservatives
February 7, 2019 · 🌐

Live in Washington, DC at the National Prayer
Breakfast with Tony Perkins of Family Research
Council.

Interviewing Tony Perkins, President -
Family Research Council at Trump Hotel in Washington DC

FREEDOM FOR THOSE WHO'VE HAD ABORTIONS

If you have had an abortion, Jesus offers complete healing at the cross. Give all guilt, shame, pain, and fear to Him, and He will cleanse and restore you. See the prayer at the end of this chapter.

What if God's total restoration allowed you to raise your child in heaven? God's love truly is stronger than death.

I've interviewed several people who have had heavenly experiences, and that is the consensus—that children we may have lost through miscarriage or abortion, we get to raise because they grow at a very slow rate compared to if they had been raised on Earth. Not only does God restore what we breach, but He empowers us to restore the breach on Earth as it is in heaven!

That's wholeness. Thank you, God.

PROTECTOR OF THE ANCIENT FOUNDATIONS—DR. KYNAN BRIDGES

Dr. Kynan Bridges had a very revelatory dream about Donald Trump. In the dream, Dr. Bridges visited President Trump at his office, and Trump gave him a thirty- to forty-pound Bible with gold gilded pages.

Dr. Bridges said that when Trump gave him the Bible, he came out of the dream, and God gave him a specific mandate to pray for Trump.

Bridges "saw that there was a cabal—this secret cabal that had been organized with a very diabolical assignment. *The assignment was to remove the ancient foundations.* The Bible actually tells us, 'Don't remove the ancient landmarks,'" Bridges said in the Facebook video.[26] I reveal more about this secret cabal in the introduction to my "Dethroning the Deep-State Prayer" at the end of this book.

He continued. "I'm talking about ancient principles and precepts in place to protect nations. . . . You see, America has never been perfect, but these ancient foundations have protected America. For example, prayer is one of these ancient foundations. The belief in the Church is an ancient foundation."[27]

In the dream, God told Dr. Bridges that He had "raised Donald Trump up, had called him to be a protector of ancient foundations. . . . There are agendas that need to be disrupted. It can only be disrupted by a disruptor. . . . I'm telling you right now, we need to pray. I saw it in a dream . . . in a vision and we must pray that the malevolent agenda of the princes of darkness would be destroyed."[28]

Bridges emphasized, **"You need to pray, you need to pray, that God's assignment to protect ancient foundations would be fulfilled."**[29]

Bridges relayed that the Bible in his dream represented the ancient foundation in our nation. He went on to say, "Things are not what they seem. Don't go by what you see. We need to get on our knees, and we need to pray. We need to seek the Lord. Put your agenda aside. Put your politics aside—whatever your persuasion aside. You are a Christian . . . and I'm telling you, if you will pray like I prayed, He will tell you what to do come this election season. . . . He will show you which way to go. You will know without equivocation. But we need to pray. . . . We need to pray for the physical safety [of Trump] and of the family. . . . When I grabbed that Bible, it was like an impartation of revelation was given to me. I knew immediately that there was a whole plan . . . I'm talking about espionage. I'm talking about treason . . . all kinds of stuff that has been brewing. And God said to me, 'I've made him to be a protector of the ancient foundations.'"[30]

I knew when I heard Dr. Bridges dream that God was confirming to me my assignment with this prayer book to preserve the ancient foundations of our nation's civil covenants—the Declaration of Independence and the Constitution. Some of the ancient foundations in Bridges's dream that the evil cabal is trying to remove are these founding documents along with major parts of history—the godly heritage parts of history.

WEEPING OVER WASHINGTON

I did not know that reading the history of George Washington in *America's God and Country* by William Federer would cause me to weep like I did.

God's repeated protection over George Washington was undeniable and brought to my remembrance the miracle stories in the Bible. I wept because it touched me that God cared for our country so much—that George Washington's faith was so strong. I loved how he prayed every morning and every night. It made me teary because of Washington's devotion to both God and country. Oh, that more of our leaders today at all levels of government would share Washington's conviction and reverence.

But then I got angry when I read that the miraculous "account of George Washington at the Battle at the Monongahela was only included in student textbooks in America until 1934."[31] Prime example of removing the ancient foundations!

Revisionist historians, or "cabal revisionists," should I say, who have stripped God out of our ancient foundations have set America on a dangerous path to destruction. Every American needs to know how God divinely protected George Washington from bullets. (Four inexplicable bullet holes were found in his coat, yet he was unharmed.) I was amazed to learn how an old Indian chief "prophesied" to Washington saying, "He will become chief of nations and a people yet unborn will hail him as the founder of a mighty empire. I am come to pay homage to the man who is the particular favorite of Heaven, and who can never die in battle."[32]

Removing miraculous divine interventions like Washington's is a perfect example of the evil assignment to remove the ancient foundations. Remember when I mentioned earlier that my husband and I brought suit against the federal government for not protecting our children in bathrooms, locker rooms, and showers? That bathroom bill lawsuit wasn't just about bathrooms; it was about removing the ancient foundations of right and wrong—of binary genders of male and female in the Bible—of the Bible's absolute morality designed to protect us by giving us clear boundaries.

The progressive left was pushing books in my county that brought gender confusion to elementary kids. They caused them to question if primary colors were really the name that had been assigned to those colors. How's that for removing an ancient boundary and creating confusion and fear? If an evil agenda to indoctrinate and brainwash our kids in elementary school can get them to question whether blue is really blue, then the evil cabal has won. Nothing is for sure. Not the sex assigned at birth. Not the primary colors that kids learn before they even learn the alphabet. Not the Bible. Not our Constitution. And certainly *not God*.

> THAT BATHROOM BILL LAWSUIT WASN'T JUST ABOUT BATHROOMS; IT WAS ABOUT REMOVING THE ANCIENT FOUNDATIONS OF RIGHT AND WRONG

We serve a loving Father who cares for His children and has provided a way of escape (1 Corinthians 10:13).

If you are not certain that you are saved, it's imperative you pray the "Prayer of Salvation" in Chapter 2 first before praying either of the following prayers.

PRAYER TO DISPEL GENDER CONFUSION

Father, Your Word tells us that we were created in Your image and that You knew us before the foundations of the earth. In Genesis 1, we see that You created us male and female, blessed us to be fruitful and multiply, and gave us dominion to rule the earth. And You saw everything that You had made, and You said it was good.

Thank you, Creator God, that *You* say that *I am good*—that I am created in *Your* image. I know, Lord, that You did not make any mistakes when You made me, for Your Word tells me that You knew me in my mother's womb, and that I am fearfully and wonderfully made!

I renounce all voices and influences of confusion that would seek to destroy my self-image. I repent of believing anything contrary to the gender You blessed me with at birth. I renounce all gender confusion and promise to rid myself of all literature, relationships, and situations that destroy my God-given identity.

Gender confusion, you have no legal right in my life. I am a blood-bought covenant believer in Jesus Christ as my risen Lord and Savior. I command you to flee from me and to cease and desist in your maneuvers to steal my identity and my destiny.

I choose to think on those things which are lovely, pure, holy, and of a good report. God, You have not given me a spirit of fear, but of power, love, and a sound mind. Because I am in covenant with Christ Jesus, I declare that I have the mind of Christ. I take every thought captive to make it obedient to Christ who loves me and gave His life for me that I might have life and have it more abundantly! In Jesus's name, amen.

Scripture References:
Philippians 4:8
2 Corinthians 10:5
John 10:10

PRAYER TO BE CLEANSED AND HEALED FROM ABORTION

Father, I repent for the shedding of innocent blood through abortion by me and by anyone in my generational bloodline. I repent for voting for any authority who advocates abortion and for participating in funding abortion in any way. I break all unholy alignments and renounce all selfishness, murder, and death. Thank You that the blood of Jesus washes me clean—white as snow—as well as my bloodline from all unrighteousness, shame, and guilt. I ask You to cleanse, heal, and restore my body from any damage that may have occurred.

Thank You for forgiving me, Father, and for restoring to me the joy of my salvation. I thank You that You make all things new. I ask You to create a clean heart in me, O'Lord, and to renew a right spirit within me. Wash my mind with the water of Your Word and help me to dwell on thoughts that are full of joy, holy, and pleasing to You, Lord. In Jesus's name, amen.

If you prayed either of these prayers, please visit my website DonicaHudson.com, and let me know. If you feel that you are in need of more godly counsel, I have counselors standing by who would love to help you.

CHAPTER 8

CALLED AND COMMISSIONED

IN THE AFTERMATH of the 2016 election and all of the chaos, murders, looting, violence, and sheer hatred, I prayed and journaled quite a bit. Here's an excerpt from my journal in 2017 where I realized that without some major changes in our culture, America was going to continue repeating this fatal pattern every election.

So what was America's problem?

THE GREAT DIVORCE

Oh, America the beautiful—there was a great divorce that took place that was never part of the covenant—the great divorce called "separation of Church and State" that was never even mentioned in My [civil] covenant.

I am calling the church government to marry the civil government anew. Yes, I am a God of remarriage, reclamation, and renewing of the covenant! As I have done with Israel so shall I do for America the beautiful.

To unseat Baal and Jezebel, the remnant must remarry.

Covenant destroys illegitimacy. It destroys the orphan spirit and fatherlessness.

In Esther 6, when King Xerxes asked for the scrolls to be read to him and found record of Mordecai alerting him to the previous assassination attempt, it was recorded on Earth as it now is in heaven through the Scriptures. When we, who are the body of Christ, make civil covenants with God, they are recorded in heaven.

~From Donica's Prayer Journal 3.22.2017

I wept as these words swept through my soul and onto the paper, feeling the very ache of a loving God whose beautiful bride is being ripped apart. Then the emotion of pain turned into righteous indignation. I am that bride! We, the Judeo-Christian Church, are that bride of Christ! It is incumbent upon us to reclaim our heritage as a Judeo-Christian nation.

God did not leave when he "married America" via multiple civil covenants. *We the people* abandoned Him. We must return to our first love—the same love of our Founding Fathers who covenanted with God and mutually pledged to each other their "Lives, their Fortunes and their sacred Honor" (Declaration of Independence).

We've seen how destitute America is in Chapters 1–7—deeply divided—at the brink of another Civil War. We've covered how Christian Americans have bought the "lie" of separation of Church and State resulting in government taking prayer out of schools in 1962 and enacting the Johnson Amendment in 1954, muzzling pastors and nonprofit Christian leaders. Americans, in general, allowed the 1978 Ethics in Government Act to neuter constitutional three-branch functionality where *we the people* have lost much of our self-governing power to unelected bureaucrats.

We've seen how U.S. political leaders and social justice organizations, often paid by George Soros's Open Society Foundation, have clandestinely carried out Alinsky's evil "rules for radicals" and moved us toward a Marxist, communist, one-world government where "America first" becomes fighting words to those yearning for the rise of the Antichrist to take his seat on the throne of the one-world government.

We've also covered the "dual citizenship" authority that Christians possess to preserve our covenant Constitution.

So how do we pray this out?

The answer lies in the word from my prayer journal—church government must marry the civil government anew.

But how?

Well, this idea of marriage representing civil covenant in Scripture is not new. God is often referred to as the husband of Israel in the old covenant.[1] In the new covenant, the Church continues to be God's bride.[2]

Covenant is the foundation of the Bible and of this nation! From Genesis to Revelation, God weaves the covenant of grace for all of the ages. Jesus fulfills the old covenant law (Matthew 5:17–20) as the seed of Abraham (Matthew 1:1; Galtians 3:16) forging a new covenant, or more aptly stated, a "re-newed covenant." Both the Greek kainos (Hebrews 8:8) and the Hebrew chadash (Jeremiah 31:31) words for "new" in new covenant translate as "renewed," rather than brand new. So God is all about re-newing covenant!

AMERICA'S GOT MARITAL PROBLEMS

Like Israel in the Bible, America's got marital problems: "Because faithless Israel had committed adultery, I gave her a certificate of divorce and sent her away. Yet I saw that her unfaithful sister Judah had no fear and prostituted herself as well (Jeremiah 3:8).

Though Israel wandered often from God, just as America does, God continually pursued a love relationship with Israel as He is pursuing one with "America the beautiful!" We are His people and the sheep of His pasture. The very writing of this book is a wooing of God to His bride, to return to Him, to be faithful!

Our Constitution was made only for a moral and religious
people. It is wholly inadequate to the government of any other.
~*John Adams*[3]

RETURNING TO OUR FIRST LOVE

Therefore, spiritually, the Church must "return to our first love" (Revelation 2:4) both personally and civically. We must realize how God has blessed our nation as our Christian Founding Fathers invoked His divine protection and blessing in our founding documents—and how He protected our Founding Fathers in battle. We must kneel to God in prayer and repentance, appealing to heaven to stop the hatred, bitterness, and injustice so that we can stand proudly in respect to our flag, honoring those who gave their lives for our freedom.

Practically speaking, *we the people* who are the Church, must run for office. We must support and vote only for candidates who will uphold the Judeo-Christian covenantal heritage of our nation so that we can become that nation described in the Declaration of Independence where "all men are created equal."

Why does the Church need to "renew our vows" of civil covenant?

For one, our very Constitution is under assault as liberals, socialists, Marxists, Muslims, and atheists now occupying office openly express desire to change our Constitution and founding documents. Publicly and verbally putting our wills in agreement with our Founding Fathers' civil covenants will usher in a force of heaven on Earth to preserve our godly heritage and save America.

God is reminding America of her covenant with Him. **God sees America as a Judeo-Christian nation, a people set aside for Him who covenanted with Him from sea to shining sea!** Like His covenant with Israel in Jeremiah 31:31, God wants to restore and renew His covenant with America—**not replace it!**

We have the best civil covenant on Earth as a republic. Like a sturdy marriage, we have stood the test of time. We remained committed to a covenant Constitution that allows for "national sins" to be purged. As mentioned earlier, former slave and abolitionist Frederick Douglass had faith that the "genius

> PUBLICLY AND VERBALLY PUTTING OUR WILLS IN AGREEMENT WITH OUR FOUNDING FATHERS' CIVIL COVENANTS WILL USHER IN A FORCE OF HEAVEN ON EARTH TO PRESERVE OUR GODLY HERITAGE AND SAVE AMERICA.

of American institutions—the constitutional system built by the Founding Fathers—would lead to the destruction of slavery."[4]

Today, I have faith that America's national sin of legalized abortion will soon be abolished under the Trump administration.

When God looks upon America, He views our nation through civil covenants that our Founding Fathers made with Him—civil covenants like the Mayflower Compact (November 21, 1620), the Mecklenburg Declaration of Independence (May 20, 1775), our national Declaration of Independence (July 4, 1776), all fifty state Constitutions, and other national and local covenants and declarations. God moved on behalf of our forefathers' prayers and covenants with Him and with each other to establish our nation.

Tragically, most of our godly heritage in history is being erased from our history books. I was *amazed* to read my daughter's fourth-grade history book the one year that I homeschooled her. I discovered that God's movement in global history that I had learned had been fully omitted from all of the secular history in public education and private education.

No wonder we are losing millennials. We have *not* been teaching them about the *empowering part* of our national history—the *God part* of civil covenant that empowers us as a nation.

Our enemy knows that if he can get America to abandon covenant with God—to divorce God as a Judeo-Christian nation—then we will be rendered powerless. We will be sitting ducks for Sharia law, socialism, and Marxism to overtake our land as we bow to foreign gods, sacrificing our unborn and "born alive" to Baal through abortion and heaping judgment upon ourselves.

IT'S TIME

If you are already saved by faith in Jesus Christ, or if you prayed the Prayer of Salvation in Chapter 2, you have met the only requirement for joining the prayer force of heaven. It's time for your commissioning oath.

OATHS ON EARTH

Both my father and my husband were in the United States Air Force. I was born on Sheppard Air Force Base in Wichita Falls, Texas, where my dad was a J.A.G. officer. When my father was commissioned as an officer, he took an oath of office to uphold the United States Constitution.

Oaths are part of the ancient foundations of society. Why do you think the communists want to ban all oaths as mentioned in Chapter 2's reading of the *Naked Communist* to Congress?

Oaths are part of the ancient foundations of the military. "All Airmen take an oath upon entry into the service. Officers take the Oath of Office upon commissioning and renew that oath with each promotion. Civilians also take an Oath of Office. Enlisted members take the Oath of Enlistment upon entry and again each time they re-enlist. . . . Oaths existed in the U.S. since early colonial days; in the 1600s, the Pilgrims established the Mayflower Compact— which served as an oath, a covenant, and a constitution."[5]

My father's Oath of Commission as a Judge Advocate General in the Air Force went like this:

I, Donald Cleveland Perry, having been appointed a Judge Advocate General in the United States Air Force, do solemnly swear that I will support and defend the Constitution of the United States against all enemies, foreign and domestic; that I will bear true faith and allegiance to the same; that I take this obligation freely, without any mental reservation or purpose of evasion; and that I will well and faithfully discharge the duties of the office upon which I am about to enter. So help me God.[6]

Although the oaths of office state that the "So help me God" part is optional, it would not have been "optional" for my dad. He was a man of faith who would have deemed the "So help me God" as the most important part.

What good is an oath if you don't invoke the help and protection of the God who created you—especially if you have to go into battle? Cancel culture would love to "cancel God" right out of our culture.

Not on my watch!

COMMISSIONED TO THE PRAYER FORCE

So, prayer warrior, are you ready to be commissioned in the prayer force of heaven and join the force of covenant and history that saves America?

Then here's your **OATH OF COMMISSION**

I, (your name), do solemnly affirm that I will support and defend the ancient covenantal foundations of my Judeo-Christian faith against all enemies; that I will bear true faith and allegiance to Jesus Christ, who gave His life for me, securing my citizenship in heaven, and that I will obey the instructions of the Holy Word of God and the Holy Spirit within me. As a praying disciple of Jesus Christ, in whom all authority in heaven and on Earth rests, I do solemnly affirm that I will support and defend the covenant Constitution of the United States in prayer against all enemies foreign and domestic; that I will pray for the president of the United States, the vice president, the Cabinet, the attorney general, and all those in authority over me that I may lead a peaceful and quiet life in all godliness and dignity. I take this obligation freely without any reservation that I might fulfill my civic duties as a Christian prayer warrior with dual citizenship and dual commandments in heaven and on Earth. So help me God.

AND HERE'S YOUR MISSION PRAYER WARRIOR

Your mission is to restore the ancient biblical foundations in America by marshalling the forces of heaven to preserve our nation.

PRAYER OF BLESSING OVER YOU

I petition our heavenly Creator on your behalf. May He endow you with great wisdom from above as you pray. May you know and feel the height and depth of His vast love for you as you war for your families, your communities, your nation, and the nations of the earth in the valley of decision.

God, I ask that each prayer warrior come to a realization of his or her full identity in Christ Jesus—that like Jesus, they would realize what they are born to do as they read Your Word, pray, and obey. I pray for each prayer warrior to feel the love and grace of Your strong presence, Lord, that they'd be quick to repent when falling short and quick to receive Your full pardon, knowing that You died for *all* of our sins, no matter how great or how small, that there is nothing that can separate them from the love of God.

I pray that no one in this "prayer force" would become disillusioned over the circumstances in the world no matter how bad, but rather, Lord, that You would open their eyes to see that those who are with us are more than those who are with them (2 Kings 6:16), that Your angelic armies are fighting on our behalf as we pray. May these prayer warriors be filled with boldness, courage, and valor as they serve You, Lord, in prayer.

I rebuke the enemy from coming to kill, steal, and destroy by commanding him to cease and desist in his maneuvers against them or their loved ones and to be gone in Jesus's name.

Thank you, Lord, that Your Word says that You protect us and that You are our rear guard.

I declare that these warriors will be strong in the Lord and in His mighty power, putting on the full armor of God so that they can stand against the devil's schemes (Ephesians 6:10–18).

I declare that these are mighty men and women of God who will hear You clearly, answer You quickly, Lord, and fall to their knees freely in prayer.

Take comfort, prayer warrior, in knowing that He hears you, He sees your faithfulness, and He is answering your prayers.

In Jesus's name, I seal this blessing. Amen.

I hope you feel loved, enlightened, and empowered to pray like never before. I've included several more specific and crucial prayers for our nation. Please stay in touch, and let me know how God answers your prayers as you join the prayer force of heaven. Visit my website at www.DonicaHudson.com to stay connected to PRAY AMERICA GREAT.

RE-COVENANTING WITH THE MAYFLOWER COMPACT

As God as our witness, just as the Pilgrims covenanted on November 11, 1620 on the Mayflower to form civil body politic for better ordering and preservation, which served as a basis for the United States Constitution and the Constitutions of all fifty states, we agree with the Pilgrims' *original intent* as "loyal subjects of our Sovereign Lord and by the grace of God," for the glory of God, and the defense and advancement of our Christian faith. We solemnly and mutually agree with the Pilgrims' civil covenant known as the Mayflower Compact, submitting ourselves one to another for justice, equality, and the common good.

Father, we recognize that the Mayflower Compact and the Pilgrim Code of Law, America's first modern constitution, were civil covenants that rested upon the consent of the governed, thereby limiting government and granting freedom to the people. We thank You that these faith-filled Christian Pilgrims pioneered a foundation for our U.S. Constitution and federal government where *we the people* are FREE—free to worship *You* in Spirit and truth, without fear of tyranny. We put our faith in agreement with theirs to preserve our FREEDOM, both governmentally and spiritually. We call upon the Church to repent of allowing government to fulfill our biblical duties, such as taking care of the poor, the widows, and the orphans.

> WITHOUT COVENANT THEOLOGY, THERE'D BE NO FEDERALISM AND NO CONSTITUTION AS WE KNOW IT TODAY.

We thank You that just as the tribes of Israel shared a covenant that made them a nation (Lutz), so does America! We thank You that the word "federal" in our federal government means *covenant*, derived from the Latin word *foedus*, and that without covenant theology, there'd be no federalism and no Constitution as we know it today.

RE-COVENANTING WITH THE HIDDEN COVENANT ROOT FOR RELIGIOUS LIBERTY AND SELF-GOVERNMENT
MECKLENBURG DECLARATION OF INDEPENDENCE, MAY 20, 1775

Father, we summon the courage of our Founding Fathers, who "risked their lives, their fortunes, and their most sacred honor" when fighting the Battle of Lexington and Concord, North Carolina, on April 19, 1775, rather than be denied the right to buy and sell or trade throughout the colonies. Today we invoke Your favor and courage to stand as our forefathers did against any form of tyranny, including globalism, microchips, injections, or vaccinations disguised with nanotechnology that would restrict our buying and selling.

DEFEATING JEZEBEL

Recognizing that the Declaration of Resolves of First Continental Congress (October 4, 1774), the Declaration of the Causes and Necessity of Taking Up Arms (July 6, 1775), and the Olive Branch Petition (July 6, 1775) held covenantal and constitutional significance because of the biblical principle of lower magistrate or interposition, we call upon *You*, Lord, to once again preserve our Constitution from tyranny and takeover by pagan ideologies like Marxism, communism, and socialism where government becomes god, and *we the people* lose our liberty and right to self-government.

Father, raise up biblical "Jehus" in America who will interpose themselves against those trying to destroy America's Constitution and religious liberty. Stop those who are trying to establish a one-world government that gives rise to the Antichrist.

Anoint and protect these "Jehus" with God-given, lawful authority to prosecute acts of treason, thereby breaking the power of Jezebel over America (2 Kings 9–10).

PRAYER TO PRESERVE CONSTITUTION—REPENT, RE-COVENANT, RESTORE

Father, in Isaiah 33:22, Your Word states, "For the Lord is our Judge, the Lord is our lawgiver; the Lord is our King; you will save us."

To keep us safe from tyranny and anarchy, we thank You that our Founding Fathers created a tripartite nature of power modelled after *You*, Lord, as Judge (our judicial branch of government), Lawgiver (our legislative branch), and King, (our executive branch). We pray for these three branches of power and that *You* would raise up godly men and women of faith to serve in Congress (Article I, Legislative Power), to serve as president and vice president (Article II, Executive Power), and as Supreme Court justices (Article III, Judicial Power) for generations to come. We pray that these men and women would be constitutionalists who embrace the original intent of the Founding Fathers to preserve religious liberty, to limit government via separation of powers and checks and balances, and to be a self-governing nation by the people, of the people, and for the people.

We thank You that our Founding Fathers recognized the depravity of man's heart as a fallen race and that *You*, Father, are the only one who holds *absolute sovereignty*. We thank You for the civil covenant of our U.S. Constitution designed to uphold these dual realities.

REPENT

On a personal level, Lord, please forgive me and cleanse me from all unrighteousness. I specifically repent of _____

_____

_____[add personal sins].

Father, on a national level, we know that judgement begins in the House of the Lord—the Church. Forgive the Church for remaining silent when prayer was taken out of schools. Forgive the Church for not standing up to the legalization of abortion in 1973. Forgive us for buying the lie of separation of Church and State because we did not know our own Constitution. Forgive us for not fighting against the portion of the Johnson Amendment in 1954 that muzzled church leaders. Forgive us for drifting away from the absolute truth and protection of God's law. Forgive us for expecting government welfare to take care of widows and orphans when Your Word clearly instructs us, Lord, that it is *our job* as the Church to do so. Forgive us for abandoning You, our first love. Forgive us for _____

_____

_____

[add other national sins].

Forgive us for embracing the dangerous lie of an "evolving, living, breathing Constitution" that changes with the interpretations of its readers. Lord, we know that this lie is rooted in a falling away from the absolute law You gave us in the Bible and upon which our Constitution was founded. Forgive us for substituting biblical absolutes with relativism leading to sociological jurisprudence.

We thank You that *You* are a God of absolute truth. You are the same yesterday, today, and forevermore. Raise up men and women who are God-fearing constitutionalists who understand federalism and the Constitution's nature as a covenant—public servants in all three branches of government who will work within the parameters of the Constitution to absolve any evils, who believe like born-again abolitionist Frederick Douglass did, that the "'genius of American institutions'—the constitutional system built by the Founding Fathers—would lead to the destruction of slavery."[7]

Forgive us for becoming drunk on independence, thinking that because *You* bestowed this great country of freedom upon us that we can therefore make up our own moral law. We as Judeo-Christians recognize that Your laws have not changed, nor will they ever change—that You provided us with a Savior in Jesus Christ who fulfilled the Mosaic Law (Ten Commandments), which served as a foundation for our nation's legal system and is engraved upon the walls and halls of many of our state's capitals.

We recognize that You created us in Your image and gave us boundaries of the law to keep us safe. We recognize that You alone, God, are sovereign over us as our Founding Fathers often stated. We thank You for Your absolute law upon which our Constitution was founded. We *reject* relative law that results in sociological jurisprudence and modern-day Marxist social justice crusades that seek to abolish our Constitution and undermine the Founding Father's original intentions.

We reject "imagined" meanings of our Constitution and pray that *You*, Lord, would put a hunger in the hearts of Americans to read, study, know, defend, and assert the Constitution.

RE-COVENANT

Father, we reaffirm our covenant with You. We thank You for cutting covenant with us by sending Your only begotten Son, Jesus, to pay the price for our sins so that we may live eternally in heaven with You. Your Word tells us that the wages of sin are death, yet while we were still sinners, Christ Jesus gave His life for us that we might inherit eternal life.

Further, we thank You for blessing our [civil] covenant Constitution and Declaration of Independence. Like the Founding Fathers who signed the Declaration of Independence, we pledge our lives, our fortunes, and our most sacred honor to each other and to You, Lord, as we ask You to save America.

RESTORE

Father, we know from Nehemiah 8–9 that on multiple occasions, the Israelite nation would repent and re-covenant with You. Subsequently, You would restore them as a nation and a people in covenant with You.

We have repented for our personal and national sins and re-covenanted with our personal and national covenants. Now we ask by faith that You would summon the forces of heaven to restore America to a covenantal paradigm of limited government and a federal republic that is interpreted through the lens of the Founding Fathers' original intentions as communicated via covenant and history. RESTORE OUR COVENANT, LORD! Restore our individual liberties that make us strong, not liberties given to our government. Raise up voices of clarity and reason among *we the people* who will point the American people to You, voices that will bring repentance and reconciliation amongst the races—repairers of the breach—who are voices that will heal the bitterness and hatred in our land with the love and healing balm of Gilead.

We honor our Founding Fathers and Mothers, which comes with a promise that we will live long on the earth (Exodus 20). We repent on behalf of Americans who have dishonored our Founding Fathers by toppling statues, rewriting history, and spreading lies designed to destroy our country.

We repent for creating a welfare system that rewards fatherlessness in America. We repent as a Church for not taking care of widows, orphans, and single mothers and expecting the government to do it. We pray for a Malachi 4 restoration of the hearts of the fathers to the children and the hearts of the children to the fathers.

INTRODUCTION TO PRAYER FOR STATE AND CONGRESS

Intro: My Facebook friend Darryl Johnson shared something on his timeline that every American needs to know so that we can pray effectively to save our country and preserve our covenant Constitution. Johnson writes,

> *Every seat in Congress was placed by the sovereignty of Almighty God, America was his dream, from the very beginning, I believe he's placed an angel over every seat, and has a perfect will for each state.*
>
> *It was never God's design, nor that of our forefathers, for an individual member of Congress to serve themselves, or any other agenda that didn't represent the people who sent them to Washington DC.*
>
> *Our country is divided among party lines and selective ideologies because the will of God that's recorded in heaven for each state isn't being done, but there's an angel standing by each seat waiting for the church to speak the Word of God over each State, in agreement with God, so that the enforcer of the covenant (the Holy Spirit) can bring about the Father's heart and selectively call those chosen to serve.[8]*

Spot on! Darryl goes on to admonish us to "pray for each seat represented in Congress, pray that God's perfect will be executed through that seat, and as we do, the angels of God, who already know what's recorded in God's book for each State, will be activated, and supernatural things will begin happening. God will be

190

prompted to move in the earth at the request of his chosen Kings and Priests, we will literally, partner up with the Godhead in prayer and bring heaven's agenda to the country, State by State, City by City, until satan has lost all political influence, and God's Kingdom begins to dominate policy and uproot wickedness."[9]

I encourage you to look up your state Constitution and any state Declarations online before praying. Focus on the parts that invoke God's name. These are the covenantal parts. Remember, God blessed America to become a land where "all men are created equal, that they are endowed by their Creator with certain unalienable rights."[10]

God blessed America with a national Constitution and state Constitutions crafted in the image of a tripartite God of King, Judge, and Lawgiver (Isaiah 33:22).

PRAYER FOR STATE AND CONGRESS

Heavenly Father, we recognize that every one of the fifty state Constitutions were stored in heaven as civil covenants when the forefathers of each state wrote them and invoked Your name. Therefore, we call upon You to reinforce these covenant constitutions as we re-covenant with You in prayer over them so that each state would fulfill Your will on Earth as it is in heaven.

Lord, we know Your plans are for good, to prosper us as a nation, to give us hope and a future (Jeremiah 29:11). We ask that where there have been breaches in civil covenants of the land, that You would restore them—that those state representatives who take oaths of office to uphold state Constitutions, the National Constitution, and America's democratic republic would either be true to their oaths of office to uphold America's form of government or be replaced by patriots and believers who will. We pray for each seat represented in state legislatures and in our national legislature. We pray that You'd endow each representative with wisdom, honesty, and integrity for the job at hand. We pray that You'd protect these representatives_____ [insert names of your representatives] and their families as they do their jobs. We pray against all self-serving agendas and for the original intent of the Founding Fathers for these representatives to be public servants who represent the people.

We ask You to empower current public servants who are legislating on Earth as it is in heaven. We ask You to call believers to run for office to replace those who won't. And finally, we ask You to wake up the Church to fulfill her civic duty and to repossess America for Your Kingdom purposes.

In Jesus's name, amen.

AGREEING WITH ABRAHAM LINCOLN—
"A PRAYER FOR OUR NATION"

Father, we put our faith in agreement with Abraham Lincoln's faith by petitioning You with his prayer:

> *Almighty God, Who has given us this good land for our heritage; We humbly beseech You that we may always prove ourselves a people mindful of Your favor and glad to do Your will. Bless our land with honorable ministry, sound learning, and pure manners. Save us from violence, discord, and confusion, from pride and arrogance, and from every evil way. Defend our liberties, and fashion into one united people, the multitude brought here out of many kindreds and tongues. Endow with Your spirit of wisdom those whom in Your name we entrust the authority of government, that there may be justice and peace at home, and that through obedience to Your law, we may show forth Your praise among the nations of the earth. In time of prosperity fill our hearts with thankfulness, and in the day of trouble, suffer not our trust in You to fail; all of which we ask through Jesus Christ our Lord. Amen.*[11]

LINCOLN'S FIRST "NATIONAL FAST DAY" SENTIMENTS:
"And whereas when our own beloved Country, once, by blessing of God, united, prosperous, and happy, is now afflicted with factions and civil war, it is peculiarly fit for us to recognize the hand of God in this terrible visitation, and in sorrowful remembrance of our own faults and crimes as a nation and as individuals, to humble ourselves before Him, and to pray for His mercy, to pray that we may be spared

further punishment, though most justly deserved; that our arms may be blessed and made effectual for the re-establishment of law, order and peace, through the wide extent of our country; and that the inestimable boon of civil and religious liberty, earned under His guidance and blessing, by the labors and sufferings of our fathers, may be restored in all its original excellence."[12]

AGREEING WITH GEORGE WASHINGTON—"PRAYER FOR AMERICA"

Almighty God: We make our earnest prayer that Thou wilt keep the United States in Thy holy protection; that thou wilt incline the hearts of the citizens to cultivate a spirit of subordination and obedience to government, and entertain a brotherly affection and love for one another and for their fellow-citizens of the United States at large. And finally that Thou wilt most graciously be pleased to dispose us all to do justice, to love mercy and to demean ourselves with that charity, humility and pacific temper of mind which were the characteristics of the Divine Author of our blessed religion without a humble imitation of whose example in these things we can never hope to be a happy nation. Grant our supplication, we beseech Thee, through Jesus Christ, our Lord. Amen.[13]

AGREEING WITH GEORGE WASHINGTON IN PERSONAL PRAYER
Sunday Morning Prayer: (From George Washington's Journal)

Almighty God, and most merciful father, who didst command the children of Israel to offer a daily sacrifice to thee, that thereby they might glorify and praise thee for thy protection both night and day, receive, O Lord, my morning sacrifice which I now offer up to thee; I yield thee humble and hearty thanks that thou has preserved me from the danger of the night past, and brought me to the light of the day, and the comforts thereof, a day which is consecrated to thine own service and for thine own honor. Let my heart, therefore, Gracious God, be so affected with the glory and majesty of it, that I may not do mine own works, but wait on thee, and discharge those weighty duties thou requirest of me, and since thou art a God of pure eyes, and wilt be sanctified in all who draw near unto thee, who doest not regard the sacrifice of fools, nor hear sinners who tread in thy courts, pardon, I beseech thee, my sins, remove them from thy presence, as far as the east is from the west, and accept of me for the merits of thy son Jesus Christ, that when I come into thy temple, and compass thine altar, my prayers may come before thee as incense; and as thou wouldst hear me calling upon thee in my prayers, so give me grace to hear thee calling on me in thy word, that it may be wisdom, righteousness, reconciliation and peace to the saving of the soul in the day of the Lord Jesus. Grant that I may hear it with reverence, receive it with meekness, mingle it with faith, and that it may accomplish in me, Gracious God, the good work for which thou has sent it. Bless my family, kindred, friends and country, be our God and guide this day and for ever for his sake, who lay down in the Grave and arose again for us, Jesus Christ our Lord, Amen.[14]

APPEAL TO HEAVEN AGAINST TREASON

Remember that God is our only sure trust.
To him, I commend you...
My son, neglect not the duty of secret prayer.[15]
~Mrs. Mary Washington to her son, George Washington

Lord, we know that American Founding Father George Washington was in covenant with You by faith in Jesus Christ as risen Lord and Savior. We thank You that he was a man of prayer who "went to church and fasted all day"[16] when seeking Your will, Lord, about whether the colonies should break ties with England.

We thank You that George Washington sought Your guidance at every juncture, flying an Appeal to Heaven flag on the Navy cruisers he commissioned during the Revolutionary War.[17] We thank You that You supernaturally protected Washington as general of the Continental Army during battles that afforded us the freedoms that we have today as a nation. Like You did for the Israelites in parting the Red Sea when fleeing from the Egyptians to the Promised Land, You caused the Catawba River in America to rise and be uncrossable for days just two hours after Washington's soldiers had crossed, preventing enemy soldiers from crossing![18] You did it again at the Yadkin River and a third time at the Dan River in Virginia, stopping the enemy from crossing on the heels of American soldiers.[19] You cloaked American troops in fog—even after the sun rose—at the East River in Long Island allowing Washington's troops to narrowly escape the British.[20] How amazing are You, Lord!

Thank You for supernaturally protecting Washington in the

Battle at the Monongahela when he had four bullet holes in his coat and two horses shot out from under him yet was not wounded at all.[21] Your Word says that You have given us the authority to trample over serpents and scorpions and over all the power of the enemy, and nothing shall by any means hurt us (Luke 10:19).

Thank You for documenting in history the prophetic words of an old Indian chief who told Washington that "a power mightier far than we, shielded you" and that Washington "will become the chief of nations and that a people yet unborn will hail him as the founder of a mighty empire."[22] You have given us, the American people, sign after sign of Your divine intervention. You blessed America to become that "mighty empire." May we recognize that all we have and all we ever will have as an empire was given to us by You!

We ask You, Lord, to restore what Washington called the "essential pillars of civil society—religion and morality"[23] and ground them in personal relationship with Jesus Christ in this country once again.

We ask Your mercy, grace, and divine deliverance for America from those who intend evil against our country.

We put our faith in agreement with Washington's faith when he wrote,

> It has always been my belief that Providence has not led us so far in the path of Independence of one nation, to throw us into the Arms of another. And that the machinations of those, who are attempting it, will sooner or later recoil upon their own Heads. HEAVEN GRANT IT MAY SOON HAPPEN UPON ALL THOSE WHOSE CONDUCT DESERVE IT [emphasis mine].

Lord, we ask You to root out the evil in our land. As Washington said, may those who are attempting to overthrow our government have their treason recoil upon their own heads. May the "Benedict Arnolds" of treason today be exposed and dealt with according to the law before harm is done to our government. As You did, Lord, for George Washington, do for us today.

> AS WASHINGTON SAID MAY THOSE WHO ARE ATTEMPTING TO OVERTHROW OUR GOVERNMENT HAVE THEIR TREASON RECOIL UPON THEIR OWN HEADS.

We remember Washington's words when the plot of Benedict Arnold to betray the Continental Army to the British was discovered. "Such an event [treason] must have given the American cause a deadly wound if not fatal stab. Happily the treason had been timely discovered to prevent the fatal misfortune. The providential train of circumstances which led to it affords the most convincing proof that the Liberties of America are the object of divine Protection."[24]

God, we ask You to continue divinely protecting our liberties and protecting our land from traitors who would not only betray our government but would betray our own children into the hands of the wicked.

Furthermore, God, we ask that You raise up godly men and women to serve in office in our nation—men and women who love You, love America, and uphold our blood-bought Constitution. Lord, we read Washington's words from a draft of his First Inaugural Address in 1789 as President of the United States:

Should . . . those incited by the lust of power and prompted by the supineness [moral weakness] or venality [corruption] of their constituents, overleap the known barriers of this Constitution and violate the unalienable rights of humanity: it will only serve to shew, that no compact among men (however provident in its construction and sacred in its ratification) can be pronounced everlasting . . . that no wall of words, that no mound of parchment can be so formed as to stand against the sweeping torrent of boundless ambition on the one side, aided by the sapping current of corrupted morals on the other.[25]

Lord, we acknowledge that we are living in those times of which Washington warned where lust of power, moral weakness, and corruption have sought to overtake the boundaries of our Declaration of Independence and our Constitution. Our unalienable rights of life, liberty, and the pursuit of happiness, along with our constitutional rights, have been trampled. The will of the people—government of the people, by the people and for the people—has been replaced with judicial tyranny and government regulation through "agencies" in many cases. The original intent of the Founding Fathers has been disregarded and discarded in an attempt to adjudicate social justice, serve special interest groups, and to line the pockets of politicians and the elite, to name a few. God, we ask that You restore the power of government back to *we the people* so that we maintain the integrity of our Constitution.

Forgive us for replacing biblical justice with social justice. Forgive us for being more concerned with pleasing man than with pleasing You, Lord. Forgive us for not knowing Your Will and Your Word concerning Israel. For YOU, Lord, are our Supreme Judge who will gather nations and bring them down to the Valley of Jehoshaphat where You judge them on behalf of Your people Israel because they have scattered them among the nations and have divided Your land (Joel 3). Forgive our country and our U.S. presidential administration for endorsing the dividing of Your land, Lord, in May of 2011 (see Chapter 3 "How We Got Here"). We know Your Word states that You will bless those who bless Israel and curse those who curse Israel (Genesis 12:3). We thank You that any curses that America received as a result of endorsing the dividing of Israel were BROKEN when President Trump acknowledged the sovereignty of Israel and the right to all of the land given her in the Holy Scriptures by moving the embassy to Jerusalem, Israel's rightful capital and covenant city. We pray that all future U.S. Presidents would follow this holy mandate of not dividing Israel which would surely result in America's land also being divided.

We also know, Father, that Your Word instructs us to pray for the peace of Jerusalem. We thank You for enabling former President Trump to sign a peace treaty with Israel and the United Arab Emirates. May this bring peace to America as well.

You are a Sovereign God who changes times and seasons, deposes kings, and raises up others. You give wisdom to the wise and knowledge to the discerning (Daniel 2:21).

Forgive us for becoming a people who do not know YOU—a people who have failed to stand up for the unalienable rights of the unborn. Forgive the Church for not speaking up when abortion was legalized and prayer was taken out of schools. Forgive us for not standing up for our unalienable right to freedom of speech when the Johnson Amendment was passed, silencing church leaders and controlling our purses. We ask You to forgive us and to restore us. In Washington's words, we ask you to forgive and to stop the "sweeping torrent of boundless ambition on the one side . . . and corrupted morals on the other."

We ask You to expose the godless lust for power of those who seek to make government our God. We renounce socialism, Marxism, communism, and Shariah law as evil forms of government that not only strip the freedom of the people, declaring government to be God, but give rise to a one-world government for the Antichrist to rule.

We declare that the God of our Founding Fathers, the God of Abraham, Isaac, and Jacob, is sovereign over America.

You and You alone, God, are the restorer of the breach. We have sinned and fallen short of the glory, Lord, but You have seen fit to restore humanity in this country. You abolished slavery through the leadership of U.S. President Abraham Lincoln. We ask You to abolish the national sin of abortion and let the healing of America begin!

In Jesus's name, amen.

AGREEMENT WITH THOMAS JEFFERSON IN NATIONAL PRAYER

[I]t becomes us humbly to approach the throne of Almighty God, with gratitude and praise, for the wonders which his goodness has wrought in conducting our forefathers to this western world . . .

[Ask] That [God} would in mercy look down upon us, pardon all our sins, and receive us into his favour; and finally, that he would establish the independence of these United States upon the basis of religion and virtue, and support and protect them in the enjoyment of peace, liberty and safety.[26]

~Thomas Jefferson, November 11, 1779

PRAYING FOR REVIVAL

Father, we seek Your Presence and the fullness thereof in the form of revival. We ask for a billion-soul harvest! We ask that You invade the nations with Your presence through skilled laborers in the field drenched in the love of God that draws men to repentance.

We ask that Your power and might would be irrefutable as men, women, and children are healed and delivered like in the New Testament days. We ask that hunger for You, Lord, for Your Word and for Your presence would sweep across this nation and wrap around the world in Jesus's name. Let it be said of America that she has regained her lampstand throughout the world—that she is once again a beacon of light for the nations to come into the Kingdom of God.

Lord, we thank You that revival is a tool to bring the nations into Christ's Kingdom and to bring reformation that secures freedom.

LET IT BE SAID OF AMERICA THAT SHE HAS REGAINED HER LAMPSTAND THROUGHOUT THE WORLD—THAT SHE IS ONCE AGAIN A BEACON OF LIGHT FOR THE NATIONS TO COME INTO THE KINGDOM OF GOD.

We thank You that the nations are Jesus's inheritance, and we are "in Jesus" through covenant.

To the one who is victorious and does my will to the end, I will give authority over the nations—that one 'will rule them with an iron scepter and will dash them to pieces like pottery'—just as I have received authority from my Father. I will also give that one the morning star. Whoever has ears, let them hear what the Spirit says to the churches (Revelation 2:26-29). Amen.

"I leave you hoping that the lamp of liberty will burn in your bosoms until there shall no longer be a doubt that all men are created free and equal."

~Abraham Lincoln

RECOVENANTING WITH THE 1607 JAMESTOWN COVENANT OF DEDICATION

Prior to praying, it is helpful to remember America's First Amendment to the U.S. Constitution:

> *"Congress shall make no law respecting an establishment of religion, or prohibiting the free exercise thereof; or abridging the freedom of speech, or of the press; or the right of the people peaceably to assemble, and to petition the government for a redress of grievances."*

Father, we know we are to pray third-heaven prayers that will cause Your Kingdom to come, Your will to be done, on Earth as it is in heaven (Matthew 6:10). In heaven, Lord, we know that we will not be silenced as believers nor prohibited from gathering to worship, nor will we be stopped from sharing our faith, sharing our trust, and sharing our love for our Lord and Savior Jesus Christ and His Holy Word. Let it be so on Earth as it is in heaven. As believers in the one who gave His life for us, WE WILL NOT BE SILENCED in the name of Jesus Christ!

We thank you, Lord, that You blessed America to evangelize the world in 1607 when America's founders at Jamestown first arrived, erected a cross, knelt, took communion, and covenanted with You, Lord, by pledging, "We do hereby dedicate this Land, and ourselves, to reach the People within these shores with the Gospel of Jesus Christ, and to raise up godly generations after us, and with these generations take the Kingdom of God to all the earth. May this Covenant of Dedication remain to all generations, as long as this earth remains, and may this Land . . . be Evangelist to the World. May all who see this Cross remember what we have done here, and may those who come here to inhabit join us in this Covenant. . . ."[27]

Father, we know that You still recognize this Jamestown generational Covenant of Dedication in heaven. We call upon You, Lord, and the hosts of heaven to enforce this covenant today in our land so that America's First Amendment rights of freedom of speech, freedom of the press, and our rights of freedom to peaceably assemble as believers in Christ would be secured and immovable. We declare that America will continue to fulfill the Great Commission and be "Evangelist to the World" in the name of Jesus!

Empower believers with boldness to stop tyrannical government that defies our First Amendment by enacting unconstitutional laws "respecting [our] establishment of religion [and] prohibit[ing] the free exercise thereof!"[28] Raise up bold leaders to push back against national and state mandates banning the assembling of churches for any reason (including COVID-19). Raise up believers to ban bills (like H.R. 5 Equality Act) which strip Christians of our First Amendment right to publicly state our deeply held religious convictions that marriage is between one man and one woman as outlined in Genesis 2:25. Empower courageous leaders to stop bills that deny free speech to Christian therapists who desire to share the love and power of Jesus Christ and freedom that God's Holy Word brings when counseling on sexual orientation. Restore free speech on Earth in America as it is in heaven so the body of Christ might be found faithful in sharing the love, hope, and freedom that life in Christ Jesus brings without fear of being jailed, censored, or banned from the public square.

We stand firmly upon your Word and upon the covenant of our founding fathers in Jamestown and "rededicate this Land and ourselves to reach the People within our shores with the Gospel of Jesus Christ." Forgive us as the body of Christ for "falling asleep" and failing to raise up "Godly generations" so that we are now having to fight to restore the freedoms we once enjoyed as Christians in America. Restore us to our first love with You, Lord, so that our Founding Fathers and Mothers from Jamestown will have blessed us with a Covenant of Dedication for America that truly "remains to all generations, as long as this earth remains" in Jesus's name.

Father, we ask that those communication platforms banning free speech either repent from censoring and banning Christians and conservatives or be replaced with platforms that will honor America's First Amendment rights to free speech.

Father, we know that "the algorithms on Google and Facebook have been trained to detect 'hate speech.'"[29] We also know that parts of Your Holy Bible have been labelled as hate speech in much of social media, mainstream media, and "woke" corporations. Father, we believe "All Scripture is God-breathed [given by divine inspiration] and is profitable for instruction, for conviction [of sin], for correction [of error and restoration to obedience], for training in righteousness [learning to live in conformity to God's will, both publicly and privately—behaving honorably with personal integrity and moral courage]" (2 Timothy 3:16, AMP). Father, we believe Your Word was born out of love to protect and guide us. Your Word also tells us that it is the loving kindness of God that draws man to repentance (Romans 2:4). Let Your followers so exhibit the loving kindness of God so that those who are lost and looking for identity in the wrong places would be drawn to us.

We who have Your Holy Spirit living within us know that You are a God of love, not hate, and that You sent Your only begotten Son, Jesus, to die for us! (John 3:16). Yours is the greatest love story ever told. We ask that You flood our state and national government leaders in the judicial, legislative, and executive branches with blood-bought lovers of Jesus and lovers of mankind who will live out the truth of the gospel with love and compassion for the lost and un-compromising biblical boundaries that bring safety to America.

Call and raise up believers to run for office in America to pre-serve the ancient foundational covenants. Call Christian attorneys to run for state offices. Call judges in the justice system to issue judicial rulings in line with Your Word. Call legislators in each state and in Washington D.C. to legislate on Earth as it is in heaven. Bring of a revival of church and state that honors You, Lord, as powerfully and humbly as the 1607 founders at Jamestown did after fleeing tyranny to establish and dedicate to You, Lord, this land known as America.

May America the beautiful remain one nation under You, Lord, with liberty and biblical justice for all, in the name of Jesus.

Amen.

DETHRONING THE DEEP STATE PRAYER

WHEN THE GREAT AWAKENING OVERTAKES THE GREAT RESET

INTRODUCTION

This may be the most critically important prayer I've ever written. If this prayer (and others like it, though I've found none) is not answered, America as we know may cease to exist. I am *compelled* to include it in this updated edition of *Pray America Great*. The earlier prayers in this book focus on saving America through constitutional covenantal prayer that mobilizes the hosts of heaven to preserve America's civil covenants while at the same time repatriating the heart of the prayer warrior. This prayer, "Dethroning the Deep State," focuses on exposing the evil seeking to destroy America's civil covenants and our love for both God and country and on praying for the Great Awakening. I encourage you to visit every link provided in the footnotes of this prayer. You will be shocked at what you find.

Since the original publication of *Pray America Great*, Americans have watched in horror as our 2020 presidential election was stolen,[30] our mainstream media and Big Tech weaponized, emerging conservative media platforms sabotaged, our energy independence surrendered, our economy sabotaged, our borders left wide open to traffickers, cartels, the COVID-infested and illegal immigrants while thousands of our own American troops and citizens were left stranded in Afghanistan. We have been stunned to learn that Biden has by default given the Taliban tens of billions of dollars ediain military weapons and supplies while causing the horrid deaths of thousands of Afghans and Americans as the men were killed, and the women and children raped and given to Taliban leaders as property.

Meanwhile, here in America, we complied, masked, and muzzled with COVID shutdowns crushing American businesses instead of crushing the coronavirus. We have watched medical tyranny keep Americans from receiving viable COVID-treatment protocols while America's frontline doctors were fired for offering treatments that work! We have watched people die by the masses—*needlessly*—through what appears to be a planned pandemic and a planned global debacle by the United States administration in Afghanistan. We have watched a democrat-controlled congress plunge America into an additional 1.5 trillion dollars in debt with an omnibus bill that our children will never be able to pay off. We have watched Joe Biden cripple American energy independence on his first day in office by shutting down the Keystone XL pipeline and "waiving sanctions on a Putin crony who leads the firm responsible for the development of the Nord Stream 2 pipeline in Europe. It's as if he wanted America to be dependent on Russia indefinitely," says North Carolina Congresswoman Virginia Foxx.[31]

This begs the question: *Who exactly is in charge here?*

Welcome to the "Great Reset," the global brainchild of the World Economic Forum (WEF), the world's richest elites who want to own and control the world. Co-parenting this feudalistic brainchild is the International Monetary Fund (IMF), the United Nations (UN), the British Royal Family, and any of us gullible enough to join the "vast network of Big Tech Corporations, online activist movements and local and national governments"[32] and Big Pharma globally pushing this agenda.

So, what is this agenda? The Great Reset is a preplanned dem-olition of the Old World Order to usher in a New World Order. In the New World Order, "You'll own nothing. And you'll be happy" and "The U.S. won't be the world's superpower. A handful of coun-tries will dominate" according to the WEF video being advertised across the U.K. and Europe.[33] These globalists are using the pan-ic and fear generated by the coronavirus bioweapon to reshape our economy and laws to destroy free market capitalism in America and force us into a new global government that focuses on bogus "net zero emissions."[34] Can you believe these narcissists want to charge us for exhaling CO2? Craftily, they have conjured a plan through eugenics to reach net zero emissions. In 2010, Bill Gates infamously laid out his sinister plan to reduce [kill] people on Earth to reach net zero emissions "through **new vaccines**, healthcare, and reproductive health services" [abortion] which he explains in his Ted Talk.[35] "The Rockefeller's Population Council and other research organizations joined with the World Health Organization (WHO) in 1972 to create a Task Force on Vaccines for Fertility Regulation. By 1995, they were able to report progress in 'developing a prototype of an anti-hCG-vaccine.' . . . The vaccine stimulates an immune reac-tion, causing women to develop antibodies against the hormone, thus preventing them from carrying babies to term."[36] British Royal Prince Charles, who favors population control, narrates the Great Reset [death plan] video as he admonishes us to "evolve our eco-nomic model."[37] Prince Charles's Father, Prince Philip, chillingly "expressed his desire to kill large numbers of people . . . stating, 'In the event that I am reincarnated, I would like to return as a deadly virus, to contribute something to solving overpopulation.'"[38]

In order to understand the broader population control agenda and how it ties into the Gates Foundation's plans, we have to look at a puzzling development that took place in 2017. In that year, Gavi—the Gates founded and funded alliance that partners the Gates Foundation, the World Health Organization, and the World Bank with vaccine manufacturers to help ensure "healthy markets for vaccines—took a strange pivot away from its core mission of vaccinating every child on the planet to providing every child with a digital biometric identity. . . ."[39] And how will this biometric identity be carried out? World Economic Forum's Yuval Noah Harari announced that "the next phase [of The Great Reset] is the surveillance going under our skin."[40] Harari is lead advisor to Klaus Schwab, the author of COVID-19 and founder of the World Economic Forum that is implementing the Great Reset.

The Great Reset represents death not only to a great swath of the human population, but also to small business and capitalism as we know it. It seeks to destroy mom and pop businesses in America (and globally), replacing them with Big Tech and Big Business. How many COVID shutdowns or future plandemics affecting public schools and universities will it take until Big Tech decides to create national and global online schools and eliminate local teachers and professors? What a much more efficient way to quickly indoctrinate masses of American youth to communism.

Under the Great Reset, business shareholders would be replaced with "stakeholders."[41] In other words, Schwab is ushering in a form of what Chief Academic Officer for American Scholars, Michael Rectenwald, calls "'corporate socialism' and Italian philosopher Giorgio Agamben has called 'communist capitalism.'"[42] Schwab's stakeholder capitalism "involves the behavioral modification of corporations to benefit not shareholders, but stakeholders—individuals and groups that stand to benefit or lose from corporate behavior."[43] That's right! The elites plan to control businesses with a social credit system straight out of the books of hellish Chinese communism, using "the Environmental, Social, and Governance (ESG) index to squeeze nonwoke corporations and businesses out of the market."[44] Not only will the planned social credit system control businesses, but it will also control humans—literally.

The Great Reset employs what Klaus Schwab deems a "Fourth Industrial Revolution." Schwab advisor, Yuval Harari, in a Google Talk speaking about humans in third person as if he is not human, defines how the Fourth Industrial Revolution will merge man and machine.

"The really big revolution, which is coming quickly, will be when the AI [Artificial Intelligence] revolution and machine learning…and infotech revolution, meets and merges with the biotech revolution and goes under the skin."[45] As if it's not alarming enough that WEF globalists like Schwab and Harari want to make us part machine to survey and control humans globally under the guise of health care, Harari openly speaks against humans having free will, referring to us as "hackable animals" and stating that "once you establish a digital dictatorship like this [global surveillance system] that has this kind of knowledge of everybody, there is absolutely no way to destroy the system from within."[46]

Earlier, I mentioned how Mr. Biden struck down America's energy independence on day one in office. I believe American oil independence is vital to preventing Americans from being controlled and swept into AI biometric transhumanism. Harari speaks often of self-driving cars which, of course, would be electric as part of the globalist "net zero emissions" farce. Self-driving cars seem inviting until you realize that the price for owning one could be allowing your brain to become part machine to interface with the electrical power grid.

One whistleblower who's distraught over what she's become through transhumanism implantable AI technology said she only had to think it, and the TV would turn on. DARPA's global health company Wellcome Leap is overtly planning to implement a trans-humanist "'in-silico' model of a child's brain to be used as the model brain that all infants will be molded to via therapeutic interventions." Wellcome Leap's "stated goal to be completed no later than the year 2030, is to have 80% of all children under the age of three monitored 24/7 with wearable devices that will read their brain patterns...."[47]

"The World Economic Forum sponsored tabletop simulations for COVID just weeks before the outbreak" and "is now doing the same for cyberattacks" which would completely shut down the power grid providing the perfect opportunity for Biden to *Build Back Better* when constructing a New World Order.[48]

In fact, at a Business Roundtable CEO Meeting, Biden warned of a "Russian Cyberattack" and fancied himself leading the New World Order stating, "There's going to be a new world order out there and we've got to lead it...."[49] Beware: Biden is already setting the stage to blame Russia for a cyberattack when Russia is actually against the globalists' Great Reset.

Most Americans do not realize that this is no longer simply Democrats versus Republicans and Marxists versus Constitutionalists. We are in a battle of globalists against nationalists. Russia and China are nationalists who are resisting the globalists' Great Reset.[50]

I am in no way advocating for nationalists like Russia and China, but I am pointing to the fact that the mainstream media is cleverly hiding the fact that Putin is fighting against globalists with special interests and bioweapon labs in Ukraine capable of killing millions in Russia. The war atrocities in Ukraine are horrible, and I pray for Ukraine. However, we must look at the entire picture globally.

When President Trump was in office, he was considered a nationalist by most of the world because he put America first and built a strong military and economy, and he protected our borders and energy independence etc. Mr. Biden is clearly a globalist Great Reset president who is putting America last in a calculated move to sweep her into the New World Order. When Biden was vice president of the United States, he spoke at the World Economic Forum in favor of global "Liberal International Order," or a New World Order, on January 18, 2017.[51]

WEF Advisor, Harari, further unveils more elite Antichrist doctrines promoting global government when he states that "the politicians will soon get into their hands the technology to create heaven or hell"[52] and that to Jews like himself, "all this story about Jesus rising from the dead and being the son of God, this is fake news"[53] which he expounds upon when discussing the notion that "God is dead" from his book *21 Lessons for the 21st Century*.[54] He further states, "Now we are acquiring divine powers of creation and destruction. We are really upgrading humans into gods. We are acquiring for instance the power to reengineer life."[55]

New World Order goals are clearly Antichrist doctrines that are anti-God, anti-human and anti-holiness (2 Thessalonians 2:3-12; Ezekiel 28; Philippians 2:6-11), which we will target in prayer.

The purpose of the New World Order is to create a one-world economy, a one-world government, and a one-world religion. Christians know that at the heart of the agenda is satan's desire to rule the world. So think twice if you think Christianity would be the "one-world religion" of the Great Reset.

Au contraire, in keeping with Marxism and global communism, Christians would be killed for continuing to worship Jesus. After all, Marx was a pagan satanist. Now we see why the deep state has been pushing Marxist ideologies like critical race theory and Black Lives Matter to breed hatred and to destroy America from within. Guess who would ultimately rule this New World Order and sit atop a global one-world government run by global elites?

That's right, ultimately, it would be the age-old foe the Bible warns us about—satan himself.

And how does the Bible warn us that satan will deceive the nations of the world?

> *The light of a lamp shall not shine in you anymore, and the voice of bridegroom and bride shall not be heard in you anymore. For your merchants were the great men of the earth, for by your PHARMAKEIA all the nations were deceived (Revelation 18:23).*

Pharmakeia is the word used in the original Greek text for Revelation 18:23. It means the use or administering of drugs, medication, poisoning, sorcery.[56] It's where we derive our words pharmacy, pharmaceutical, and "Big Pharma."

Dr. Michael McDowell warns that not only is the COVID-19 vaccine a genetic bioweapon, but that we are in a "new kind of arms race" where currently "60 nations stockpile genetic bioweapons." Dr. McDowell reveals that "Big Pharma owns and controls media, the World Health Organization, U.S. Legislature, medical research journals, scientific journals, medical schools, national governments, public health authorities, medical fraternities, media, the business sector, ecclesiastic leaders"... where the "ELECTED, ELITES and ECCLESIASTICS have bonded together to vaccinate the world."[57]

Big Pharma, Big Tech news media, and the U.S. Government lied to the American people about the safety of COVID vaccines. Worse yet, our government is preparing to force these shots through "vaccine passports!"[58]

Liberty Counsel reports, "As early as February 28, 2021, Pfizer knew the incredible damage its shot was inflicting on Americans. Even worse, the FDA also knew and tried to hide these and many other facts from you. Instead of telling the truth, our government spent 1 billion of your tax dollars to brainwash people to get this injection . . . and then forced this shot onto millions more. . . . At least 26,396 reported deaths have been associated with these shots, plus an additional 4,423 miscarriages. Almost 49,000 people have been permanently disabled. And more than 1.2 million people have had adverse reactions."[59] Furthermore, "nanotechnology is currently being used in two of the three mRNA COVID-19 vaccines being given in the United States today.[60] The fact that a bioluminescent ingredient named "Luciferase" which alters our RNA or DNA is in the Moderna COVID vaccine should be enough to cause any Christian to search out the truth before getting a vaccine or boosters number 2, 3, 4, 5 ad infinitum!

Dr. Carrie Medej warns . . . that the COVID injections have two purposes: 1. to reprogram our DNA to make us human–AI hybrids that are easier to control and 2. to implant a Digital Vaccine ID that will allow total control over each person. Dr. Carrie Madej reveals how Big Tech collaborates with Big Pharma to introduce new technologies in the vaccines that will alter our DNA and turn us into hybrids. This will end humanity as we know it, and start the process of transhumanism: HUMAN 2.0. The plans are to use vaccines to inject nanotechnology into our bodies and connect us to the Cloud and artificial intelligence. This will enable corrupt governments and tech giants to control us without us being aware of it. [61]

Make no mistake, PHARMAKEIA is the demonic spirit that satan is using through genetic bioweapons, synthetic human genome altering vaccines, and nanotechnology in foods and vaccines to control the nations. "According to many experts in the United States, there are 1,900 to 2,500 food products that use nanotechnology."[62] Nanotechnology in vaccines, foods, and medicines makes communistic biometric surveillance possible and moves us rapidly into transhumanism.

"COVID is critical because this is what convinces people to accept, legitimize total biometric surveillance. If we want to stop this epidemic, we need not just to monitor people, we need to monitor what's happening under their skin" says Yuval Harari, aforementioned lead advisor of the WEF Great Reset, noting that he would have liked to "have known that he was gay" when he was younger instead of at age twenty-one and that "today . . . any algorithm of Microsoft or Amazon or the government would be able to know such a thing when [he] was twelve or thirteen just by monitoring what's in [his] body . . ."[63]

"If Big Tech's capabilities are allowed to develop unchecked and unregulated, these companies will eventually have the power not only to suppress existing political movements, but to anticipate and prevent the emergence of new ones. This would mean the end of democracy as we know it and place us under the thumb of an unaccountable oligarchy." according to Allum Bokhari, senior technology correspondent at Breitbart News.[64] Big Tech's role in advancing the Great Reset is huge.

In an October 2020 open letter to President Donald Trump that went viral before the November 2020 presidential election, Ulpiana Archbishop Carlo Maria Viganò warned of the destructive Great Reset that had already been financed in several nations, stating that "The *Great Reset* is the imposition of a health dictatorship aiming at the imposition of liberticidal measures, hidden behind tempting promises of ensuring a universal income and cancelling individual debt. The price of these concessions from the International Monetary Fund will be the renunciation of private property and adherence to a program of vaccination against COVID-19 and COVID-21 promoted by Bill Gates with the collaboration of the main pharmaceutical groups. Beyond the enormous economic interests that motivate the promoters of the *Great Reset*, the imposition of the vaccination will be accompanied by the requirement of a health passport and a digital ID, with the consequent contact tracing of the population of the entire world. Those who do not accept these measures will be confined in detention camps or placed under house arrest, and all their assets will be confiscated."[65]

CHAPTER 8: CALLED AND COMMISSIONED

In case you think this was too far out, on August 6, 2021, Tennessee Governor Bill Lee signed Executive Order No. 83 authorizing the military to assist with COVID Testing and to "operate public or privately owned" ambulances to "hospitals, emergency departments, and **alternate care sites . . .**"[66]

"The Tennessee EO is on top of the CDC's announcement that COVID camps will be set up on a nationwide basis, with people being medically kidnapped and taken to 'humanitarian settings' . . ."[67] The National Guard posted job openings for "Internment/Resettlement Specialists" on July 15, 2021 at camps mostly near prisons in thirteen states, including Tennessee, where civilians can be interned "for their protection" according to an Obama Administration Department of Defense directive.[68]

Make no mistake. These types of internment camps are for the well, not the sick as you'd think. The CDC (Center for Disease Control) calls it the "shielding approach" where "people deemed high-risk, like the elderly and those with underlying conditions, would be temporarily relocated to safe or 'green zones' established at the household, neighborhood, camp/sector, or community level, and would have minimal contact with family members and the surrounding community."[69] Of course "important alterations to religious practice, custom and tradition will be imperative" at these camps.[70]

Hasn't this been satan's goal all along anyway—to separate and stop believers from worshipping God?

This may seem like a lot of heavy information at one time, but none of this has caught God by surprise. In fact, He has warned us all along through Scripture and equipped us for the battle at hand and for any future "plandemics"! There is a lot we can do, both on our knees mobilizing the hosts of heaven and through exposing this evil agenda so that good-hearted Americans can turn this country around with God's help. This is the *only* way *we the people* of America will maintain our constitutional republic and our freedom to worship Jesus. That's why we must also pray for a Great Awakening so that the eyes of Americans will be opened to the global plot to destroy us and the hearts of Americans will be open to receiving the love of Christ and His divine eternal protection.

God in His love for mankind gave us a roadmap in the Scriptures to prepare us for the times we face today. May this prayer activate your Holy Spirit GPS as you navigate through the days and years ahead.

Know that through Jesus Christ and His eternal sacrifice, our heavenly Father has given all we need to be victorious.

Welcome to the *Prayer Force!*

PROPHETIC WORD OF ENCOURAGEMENT
"*THE DAYS OF RECKONING ARE AT HAND*, says the Lord. *For I will pour out my spirit upon all flesh and blood in these last days . . .*" (Joel 2:28) with dreams and visions, revelation, and mass population of kingdom warriors who will not cease praying and taking dominion over the powers of darkness seeking to hasten the demonic New World Order.

"Only the saints can hasten the coming of My Son," says the Lord. "Demonic attempts to hasten the New World Order will be foiled as My saints rise up in prayer to hasten the Great Awakening! **Awakening** will OVERTAKE the **reset**," says The Lord. "For I am returning for a bride without spot or blemish. Her lamp will be full of the oil of My Holy Spirit. She will be awaiting Me at the time of My return. She will not fall for an impostor groom nor will she fail to hear My voice, for she knows Me. She knows My Word as a lamp unto her feet and a light unto her path (Psalm 119:105), and she will not be fooled by a false light. For Jesus is the light of the world! (John 8:12).

Cheer up! For Jesus has overcome the world! (John 16:33)."

DECLARATION

We declare in the name of Jesus that we have eyes to see and ears to hear as biblical prophecy from Your Holy Word is fulfilled. Fear is not our guide, and the arm of flesh is not our savior (Jeremiah 17:5). The Lord Jesus Christ is!

We hearken to Your Holy Spirit within us. We incline our ears to Your truth for You will guide us into peace. You have a remedy for every attack we have suffered and ever will suffer. You are the Great I Am, the Great Physician, Jehovah Rapha, our Healer, our Waymaker, our Strong Tower. You did not come to Earth to rescue willful traitors who refuse You, but You came to offer salvation to those who choose You.

We choose this day whom we will serve. You have put before us life and death. We choose life! We will choose wisely over the false gods of this world and over any false gods of our ancestors! We say, ". . . but as for me and my house, we will serve the Lord!" (Joshua 24:15). We thank you for household safety, protection, joy, and peace to all who dwell with us in Jesus's mighty name!

We declare that the sinless blood of Jesus is more powerful than satan for it has given Jesus all authority, power, and sovereignty (Matthew 28:18). Jesus shed His sinless blood for *all* mankind, that those who believe in Him will have eternal life (John 3:16). Those who disregard His perfect sacrifice will reap eternal damnation (Matthew 25:46).

Lord, we also recognize that You are not willing that any should perish (2 Peter 3:8–10) but that *all* would come to the knowledge of Jesus Christ as the risen Lord and Savior of mankind.

We declare that many will renounce their service to the Luciferian New World Order in the name of Jesus and receive everlasting life in Christ Jesus.

We declare that Jesus, the Messiah, has fulfilled the Old Covenant (Ten Commandments). We declare, according to Exodus 20, that we will have no other gods before You, Lord (vs. 3), that we shall not make and worship any carved image or any likeness of anything that is in heaven above or that is in the earth beneath or that is in the water under the earth. You are a jealous God visiting the iniquity of the fathers on the children to the third and fourth generations of those who hate You but showing steadfast love to thousands who love You and keep Your commandments (vs. 4–6).

PRAYER OF REPENTANCE/CLEANSING BLOODLINES

I repent of having believed any lies of the enemy. I repent of all my sins including any involvement with the occult, the New World Order, and/or the Great Reset. I thank You, Father, that Jesus Christ shed His sinless blood for me that I might have eternal life by receiving Him as my risen Lord and Savior.

I ask Jesus to send His Holy Spirit to dwell within my heart. I thank you that I am now part of Jesus's family. His sinless bloodline has now replaced and atoned for all sinful bloodlines of my forefathers in me.

I plead Jesus's blood over my children and my children's children down to the third and fourth generations. I declare that my bloodline loves You and keeps Your commandments, Lord, and that we shall receive Your steadfast love both now and forevermore in Jesus's name (Exodus 20:6).

PREPARING FOR BATTLE PRAYER

In the name of Jesus, as we prepare to battle through prayer, we put on our full armor according to Ephesians 6. We suit up with the helmet of salvation, the breastplate of righteousness, the belt of truth, the gospel shoes, the shield of faith, and the sword of the Holy Spirit. We plead the blood of Jesus over our minds, wills, and emotions, asking that You, Lord, give us wisdom and discernment for the days ahead.

We take authority over fear right now in Jesus's name. We say that fear of COVID1-9 and it's variants, fear of vaccinations, fear of vaccine passports, fear of medical tyranny, fear of death, fear of communism, Marxism, socialism, and Satanism, fear of the New World Order, fear of_____[fill in blank] must leave in Jesus's name. For You have not given us a spirit of fear but a spirit of POWER, LOVE, and a SOUND MIND (2 Timothy 1:7).

We will not make decisions out of fear, and we cast down all demonic brainwashing, mind-control techniques, and spirits designed to control us in Jesus's name. Instead, we call upon Your Holy Spirit to lead and guide us into all truth (John 16:13) as Your peace, which passes all understanding, guards our hearts and our minds in Christ Jesus (Philippians 4:7).

BATTLE PRAYER

NOTE: You will see in the following prayers that strongholds or demonic platforms are named in detail. This is because as we pray, we are literally pointing the armies of heaven at the targeted demonic strongholds we wish to tear down.

Many Christians think that when we pray, we are just throwing words into the universe, hoping something sticks. They are not sure really that God hears them. We need to understand that not only does God hear us, but He also has assigned the heavenly hosts to assist us when we pray (1 John 5:14-15).

Through Christ Jesus, God has given believers the authority on Earth. Our responsibility is to pray God's will and His Word over situations that do not line up with heaven so that we would see "[His] kingdom come, [His] will be done, on Earth as it is in Heaven" (Matthew 6:10).

Dear Heavenly Father, we recognize that You created the heavenly hosts to protect, guard, and fight on our behalf! Your Word tells us in Isaiah 13:4-5, "…The Lord of Hosts is mobilizing an army for war. They come from faraway lands, from the ends of the heavens—the Lord and the weapons of His wrath—to destroy the whole country" (BSB).

Father, we recognize that Your heavenly armies are more powerful than any armies of the nations of the earth. We also know from Your Word that Jesus Christ is LORD of HOSTS (Colossians 2:10). Therefore, because we are citizens of heaven and joint heirs of Christ, we take authority over *all* the power of the enemy (Luke 10:19). We call for the heavenly armies to fight on our behalf to destroy the globalists' satanic agenda known as the "Great Reset." We recognize that the Great Reset is a declaration of war against America's constitutional republic and the fundamental liberties of every American. We further recognize that the Great Reset is trying to destroy the nations of the world economically, militarily, and spiritually to move us into a one-world communistic government where government is god and Christians are killed. We know the goal of the Great Reset is to prepare the world to be ruled by the Antichrist through a one-world government, a.k.a. New World Order (NWO).

Lord, You have not called us just to sustain and occupy, but You have called us to advance the Kingdom of God on this earth as long as we have breath by sharing the love of Christ that draws all men to repentance (Matthew 28:16–20).

You have given us all authority through our blood covenant with Jesus Christ "to trample on serpents and scorpions and over all the power of the enemy and nothing shall by any means hurt us" (Luke 10:19). You have given us jurisdictional authority as citizens of America to preserve our constitutional republic and our religious liberty.

We see how deep-state globalists have used the COVID crisis to usher in the Great Reset. We will not shut down our churches out of fear and stop worshipping You, Lord. Your Word tells us that even the rocks will cry out if we keep silent!

We will not shut down our businesses! We will use our weapons of warfare, which are not carnal but are mighty to the pulling down of strongholds (2 Corinthians 10:4) to marshal the armies of heaven to preserve our divine right to worship You, Lord, freely and to self-govern.

We also recognize You created all men equal. There is neither Jew nor Greek, slave nor free, male nor female, for we are all one in Christ Jesus (Genesis 1:27; Galatians 3:28). Therefore, we call upon the armies of heaven to destroy all Great Reset platforms that seek to divide us into a feudal system of global elites who own everything and "we the plebians" who own nothing.

Shred those spiritual platforms so that those being controlled by Antichrist spirits of segregation, racism, elitism, totalitarianism, communism, Marxism, and socialism will be destroyed over our nation and over all nations seeking to implant these demonic forces in America.

Lord, we recognize that the spirit of Antichrist is behind the so-called Great Reset. This Antichrist, or man of lawlessness, is also **anti-God, antihuman,** and **antiholiness** (2 Thessalonians 2:3–12; Ezekiel 28; Philippians 2:6-11).

> *1 John 2:18* — *Little children, it is the last time: and as ye have heard that antichrist shall come, <u>even now are there many antichrists</u>; whereby we know that it is the last time (KJV).*

> *Mark 13:21* — *And then if any man shall say to you, Lo, here is Christ; or, lo, he is there; <u>believe him not: (KJV).</u>*

> *Mark 13:22* — *For false Christs and false prophets shall rise, and shall shew signs and wonders, to seduce, if it were possible, even the elect (KVJ).*

> *Mark 13:23* — *But take ye heed: behold, I have foretold you all things (KJV).*

We pray for the spirit of lawlessness in America to be broken. We ask that you establish a spirit of justice and peace in America, raising up godly leaders in our country to carry this out.

DEFEATING ANTI-GOD ANTICHRIST SPIRITS

Lord, we take power over *all* the power of the enemy (Luke 10:19) operating in the demonic platform of the New World Order in America and in other countries which seek to destroy America. Our Founding Fathers risked their lives, their fortunes, and their most sacred honor to secure America's liberty when they called upon You, Lord, to bless the civil covenants of our U.S. Constitution, Declaration of Independence, Mayflower Compact, all fifty state constitutions, and more.

We the people of America made civil covenants with You, Lord, *not with the devil.* Therefore, we send the hosts of heaven to pull down every plot, plan, attack, threat of terrorism, threat to religious liberty, threat of destruction to America's Constitution, and any deceit perpetrated against the American people by the Antichrist, anti-God New World Order spirits including Satanism, Luciferianism, Illuminati, high-level Freemasonry, Marxism, communism, and various forms of witchcraft and the occult. Confuse their demonic camps. Shred the platform that the New World Order operates from in America. Pull down these strongholds controlling people in our government, media, entertainment industry, churches, educational systems, healthcare systems, political parties, and families. Remove these demonic spirits from our country in Jesus's name.

We renounce the WEF's lie that "government owns all and provides all."[71] We also renounce the Great Reset goal "to take away individual ownership of all property and place it in the hands of a world government" as stated in a World Economic Forum video.[72] We renounce "defunding of the police" and the move to disarm Americans by the left and by the United Nations Office for Disarmament Affairs as a globalist setup for America to be run by the United Nations' global police force for a one-world government. [See "Appendix, Current Communist Goals" #11.]. We employ the hosts of heaven to tear down these demonic structures of global elite ownership and lawlessness in the name of Jesus.

We declare that You, Lord Jesus, are Lord of all, for the earth is the Lord's and all it contains (1 Corinthians 10:26). Government is NOT God, and government never will be God in America. We depend upon You, Lord, for all of our provision and freedom. We declare that America's covenantal Constitution shall stand on Earth as it is recognized in heaven.

We declare that the father of lies has overplayed his hand in seeking to hasten the New World Order/one-world government and creating deceptive lies through mass media. He is a defeated foe! We send the hosts of heaven to break off the spirit of mind control and fear and to expose the plots of the enemy. We are not afraid for we know that those who are with us fighting for our constitutional freedoms are more than those who are with the New World Order seeking to destroy America.

Open our eyes as You did in the days of Elisha (2 Kings 6:17), Lord, that we may see the land full of the angelic army's chariots of fire fighting to preserve our republic.

Blessed is the nation whose God is the Lord! (Psalm 33:12).

DEFEATING ANTIHUMAN ANTICHRIST SPIRITS

Lord, your Word declares in Genesis 1:26–27,

> *Then God said, "Let us make man in our image, after our likeness. And let them have dominion over the fish of the sea and*

over the birds of the heavens and over the livestock and over all the earth and over every creeping thing that creeps on the earth." So, God created man in his own image, in the image of God he created him; male and female he created them.

Lord, we recognize that we were created in Your image and set apart to commune with You and to rule and reign with You. We are in awe at the sanctity of the human life that You have bestowed upon us. We are astounded that You loved mankind so much that You would cause Your only begotten Son, Jesus, to take the form of the "second Adam" to secure our eternity in heaven and to restore our authority on Earth after the first Adam fell.

Therefore, we take authority over *all* the power of the enemy (Luke 10:19) operating in the New World Order antihuman demonic spirits. We send the hosts of heaven to deconstruct and shred the platform of the antihuman "Fourth Industrial Revolution" that merges man and machine for the ultimate purpose of controlling, programming, and moving mankind into accepting implantable cryptocurrency technology to buy, sell, and trade in the Antichrist New World Order.

Revelation 13:16–18 ISV - The second beast forces all people important and unimportant, rich and poor, free and slaves— to be marked on their right hands or on their foreheads, so that no one may buy or sell unless he has the mark, which is the beast's name or the number of its name. In this case wisdom is needed: Let the person who has understanding calculate the total of the beast, since it is a human multitude, and the sum of the multitude is 600, 60, and six [666].

We command the hosts of heaven to pull down every strong-hold and demonic plot to force humans to buy, sell, and trade in the world banking system with Bill Gates's EMBEDDABLE cryptocurrency technology (patent **060606**)[73] and Gates's IMPLANTABLE microchip "quantum dot tattoos" to identify vaccinated and unvaccinated[74] and to deliver vaccines using biolu-minescent Luciferase.[75] Tear down any antihuman Antichrist spir-itual platforms merging man and machine *for the purpose of demise or control*, including electromagnetic poisonous graphene oxide nanotechnology in COVID-19 vaccines[76] and DARPA hydrogel.[77]

We send the hosts of heaven to expose and pull down the strongholds and sinister plots within transhumanism and artificial intelligence. We declare that artificial intelligence and true vac-cines will only be used for good and not to harm mankind.

Expose the architects of the Great Reset, the Fourth Industrial Revolution, transhumanism, artificial intelligence, 5G-activated graphene oxide nanotechnology, DARPA hydrogel, luciferase in vaccines, global eugenics through vaccine and abor-tion, COVID-19 bioweapon, climate change, and all other anti-human, anti-God constructs of the New World Order. We send the hosts to pull down the strongholds controlling these architects and those carrying out the sinister agendas. We send the hosts of heaven to destroy the platform of human trafficking, satanic ritual abuse, adrenochrome production and distribution, abortion, fetal aborted cells in vaccines, and every evil antihuman abuse feeding "the beast" (Revelation 13:16–17).

We expose and renounce the lie that it's okay if a baby is sac-rificed (through abortion) to give humanity fetal cells for a vaccine.

JESUS was our perfect sacrifice! Jesus gave us power and authority over all demons and power to cure diseases (Luke 9:1–2). Therefore, we pray for healing of the masses who have been hit with the COVID-19 bioweapon. We call for the evil platform of abortion in America to be destroyed and for the healing of all women and men who have repented of abortion. Turn those who have repented from victims into victor warriors! You are a loving God who cleanses, heals, and empowers all who come to You with repentant hearts.

We call for the hosts of heaven to reinforce the globally accepted 1947 Nuremburg Code in which "The voluntary consent of the human subject is absolutely essential." Destroy all demonic platforms and every lofty thing that seeks to steal human consent for vaccines including the COVID-19 vaccine in Jesus's name. We declare that we will not be human experiments in Jesus's name, nor will we be conditioned to conform to a satanic plot that prepares us to take the mark of the beast in the future (Revelation 13:16–18).

Lord, we recognize that Great Reset eugenics and population control are antihuman products of a satanic, narcissistic, psychopathic mindset seeking to "kill, steal, and destroy" humanity (John 10:10). We further recognize that the climate change movement within the Great Reset is being used to *play God* by perpetrating the lie that there's too much CO2 on the planet; therefore, the population needs to be lowered "through new vaccines, healthcare, and reproductive health services" [abortion] as Bill Gates states in his "Ted Talk"[78] and **taxed** on the CO2 gas we exhale ("carbon pricing") as International Monetary Fund boss Kristalina Georgieva states.[79] Therefore, we call upon the hosts of heaven to tear down the demonic strongholds of narcissism, psychopathy, sociopathy, witchcraft, genocide, and crimes against humanity operating through individuals controlling nations, corporations, abortive healthcare organizations like Planned Parenthood, agencies like the IMF (International Monetary Fund), WEF (World Economic Forum), UN (United Nations), and bloodline families of the deep state.

We fully recognize the demonic Babylonian spirit of "pharmakeia" deceiving the nations of the world and pushing them into an end-time New World Order. We call the hosts of heaven to destroy the stronghold of pharmakeia over media, the World Health Organization, U.S. Legislature, medical research journals, scientific journals, medical schools, national governments, public health authorities, medical fraternities, media, the business sector, ecclesiastic leaders, elites and elected officials. Shred into pieces the false pharmakeia trinity of the ELECTED, ELITES, and ECCLESIASTICS seeking to impose lockdowns, forced genetically altering vaccinations, vaccine passports, internment camps, etc. in Jesus's name.

We ask you, Lord, to raise up Americans to enforce the 1989 Bioweapons Anti-Terrorism Act to protect our country from further bioweapons. We send the hosts to foil future attempts of deep-state globalists to terrorize our country with bioweapons. We pray for the reversal of the Direct To Consumer Law (DTC Law) that opened the floodgates for pharmakeia to control America by advertising prescriptions drugs directly to the public. We send the hosts of heaven to stop the censoring of science in Jesus's name.

We renounce the diabolical historical pattern of how the deep state creates crises like coronavirus[80] and "capitalizes off crises to consolidate control."[81]

We call upon the hosts of heaven to break the deep-state witch-craft pattern of creating crises through wars, famines, weather catastrophes, disease, plagues, etc. over America. We call upon the hosts to dismantle the platform of medical tyranny with COVID-19, to expose and punish those who are withholding viable medical treatments from humanity, and to expose and punish those who are poisoning humanity through vaccines.[82]

We send the hosts to release viable cures and medicines like Ivermectin, Hydroxychloroquine, and proven frontline doctor protocols currently being withheld from the American people. We command the hosts to tear down and foil all plans to prohibit over-the-counter immunity boosting supplements like zinc and quercetin from being available to the public.

Dismantle all plots to create food shortages, to create government dependence (socialism) by paying American workers more money to stay home than go to work, to shut down businesses and churches due to fear of COVID, to separate the vaccinated and the unvaccinated, to separate and mask people six feet apart according to satanic ritual.[83]

We renounce the "occult transformation . . . from *individual sovereign* under God to *collective subject* under the children of the devil."[84]

We further renounce Great Reset front man Klaus Schwab's vow in his book on COVID and the Great Reset that "life would 'never' return to 'normal'" and Schwab's reference to "before coronavirus (BC)" and "after coronavirus (AC)"! We renounce these lies in the name of Jesus. We declare that only ONE God split time into BC and AD. His name is JESUS!

We further declare that a deep-state bioweapon designed to condition humanity for global feudalism will *not* supplant our risen Lord and Savior, Jesus Christ. We call for the hosts to tear down witchcraft spirits of deceit, manipulation, domination, intimidation, and fear of dying, fear of COVID, fear of pandemics, and false promises of "'peace' and 'safety' that will never be fulfilled."[85]

We take authority over the demonic reeducating and reengineering platforms of the Great Reset in the areas of industry, society, education, agriculture, relationship, and even under the skin of human beings, and we command them to leave in Jesus's name.[86] We further take authority over the sinister plot to use internment camps for Americans! We send the hosts of heaven to expose and overturn every evil internment camp plot, gubernatorial executive order, and governmental regulation by the CDC, WHO, and Big Pharma state by state in the name of Jesus.

We pray for America to once again become energy independent. Specifically, we pray against all globalist plots seeking to cripple America's energy independence, sink us fiscally with trillions more in debt, destroy our police force, ruin our military, flood our borders with terrorists, traffickers, and cartel to be exposed and demolished in Jesus's name.

DEFEATING ANTIHOLINESS ANTICHRIST SPIRITS

Lord, Your Word tells us that we are to be holy as You are holy (morally blameless). Father, in Jesus's name, we take power over *all* the power of the enemy operating in the Antichrist, antiholiness spirits in America. We send the hosts to destroy the platforms of demonic division and hatred toward America, hatred toward our Founding Fathers, hatred toward God, hatred toward parents, hatred toward God-given binary genders of male and female, hatred of one's own gender, hatred between races, hatred toward authority, etc. We renounce transgenderism as a form of witchcraft worship of Baphomet who has both male and female sexual organs.

We call upon the hosts to destroy witchcraft platforms, organizations, and industries promoting sexual immorality (1 Corinthians 6:18; 1 Thessalonians 4:3), gender confusion, promiscuity, pornography, pedophilia, prostitution, sexual abuse, human trafficking, beastiality, lust, identity confusion, homosexuality, and sodomy in the name of Jesus (1 Corinthians 6:9; Jude 1:7).

We command the hosts of heaven to go and destroy the spiritual platforms of corrupt teachings in America's educational system. In Jesus's name, destroy the evil platforms of "comprehensive sexual education" in our children's schools that are teaching, illustrating, and often showing videos of such debauchery as transgender organ mutilation, masturbation, promiscuity, illicit sexual acts, homosexuality, pedophilia, and other unholy acts designed to desecrate and indoctrinate our children. Replace these unholy curriculums and those who teach them with God-fearing, holy educators who love God, our country, and our children and with curriculums that are historically accurate, holy, and devoid of indoctrination.

In Jesus's name, we command the hosts to destroy the platform of satanic Marxism and communism in America perpetrated by the deep-state network of trained Marxists infiltrating our culture with critical race theory (CRT) and Black Lives Matter (BLM). Shred spiritual platforms of racial division and segregation rooted in Marxist "critical theory" in Jesus's name.

We cast down all skin-color shaming, segregation, hatred, and elitism in Jesus's name. We declare that the people of God will be known by their love one for another regardless of skin color, nationality, and socioeconomic status in the name of Jesus.

We command the hosts of heaven to destroy all unholy platforms of deceit, lies, sabotage, trickery, treason, bribery, blackmail, and dishonesty in all fifty states in America's judicial, executive, and legislative branches, in Big Tech and mainstream media, in America's electoral process, in businesses, in agencies like the CIA and FBI, police forces, and in America's armed forces. May truth, righteousness, and grace in Christ Jesus prevail in these organizations in Jesus's name.

We command the hosts of heaven to seek out and destroy the evil platform of unholy satanic ritual abuse and human/child trafficking in America and in the deep state globally. Destroy and smash to pieces the demonic stronghold of witchcraft and child sacrifice feeding the beast at the altar of Molech (2 Kings 23:10, 16:3, 21:6; Jeremiah 32:35; Leviticus 20:2–5). Destroy the unholy despicable spiritual platform of mind control in America including MK Ultra programming, Sex Kitten programming, Project Monarch, Betas (sexually programmed slaves), Illuminati mind control, transhumanism, dehumanization, mind control, altered personalities, MK Delta programming, and others. We declare Isaiah 26:3, "Thou wilt keep him in perfect peace, whose mind is stayed on thee: because he trusteth in thee."

So if there is any encouragement in Christ, any comfort from love, any participation in the Spirit, any affection and sympathy, complete my joy by being of the same mind, having the same love, being in full accord and of one mind. Do nothing from selfish ambition or conceit, but in humility count others more significant than yourselves. Let each of you look not only to his own interests, but also to the interests of others. Have this mind among yourselves, which is yours in Christ Jesus, who, though he was in the form of God, did not count equality with God a thing to be grasped, but emptied himself, by taking the form of a servant, being born in the likeness of men. And being found in human form, he humbled himself by becoming obedient to the point of death, even death on a cross. Therefore God has highly exalted him and bestowed on him the name that is above every name, so that at the name of Jesus every knee should bow, in heaven and on earth and under the earth, and every tongue confess that Jesus Christ is Lord, to the glory of God the Father (Philippians 2:1–11 ESV).

Finally, brethren, whatsoever things are true, whatsoever things are honest, whatsoever things are just, whatsoever things are pure, whatsoever things are lovely, whatsoever things are of good report; if there be any virtue, and if there be any praise, think on these things (Philippians 4:8 KJV).

AWAKENING PRAYER

"And [the Angel] said, Go thy way, **Daniel**: for **the words** *are* **closed up** and **sealed till the time of the end.** Many shall be purified, and made white, and tried; but **the wicked shall do wickedly**: and none of the wicked shall understand; **but the wise shall understand**" (Daniel 12:9, 10 **KJB**).

We declare that we are the wise who understand the times.

We pray that Your Church would awaken to the knowledge of Jesus Christ as our risen Lord and Savior and would become spiritually attuned to the end-time war being waged upon our culture right now in the name of Jesus. We pray for repentance from spiritual slumber, stupor, apathy, and complacency now in Jesus's name. We pray for unity in the body of Christ that commands a blessing.

We take authority over *all* power of the enemy and send the hosts to rip the veil of deceit off the eyes of the slumbering bride in America. Send an Issachar anointing to your bride to make her aware of the times and seasons so that she would not miss her visitation and would yearn to be with her groom! Even so, come Lord Jesus!

This is the confidence we have in approaching God: that if we ask anything according to his will, he hears us. And if we know that he hears us—whatever we ask—we know that we have what we asked of him (1 John 5:14-15).

Lord, we thank You for our authority in Christ Jesus. We thank the army of Christ Jesus for being faithful to preserve our country for His Kingdom purposes. We thank You that You have heard our prayers, Lord, and are destroying the Antichrist, anti-god, antihuman, antiholiness demonic platforms in the name of Jesus!

We recognize that the Great Reset move toward a New World Order/one-world government is a direct attempt by satan to strip Jesus, the Messiah, of His rightful inheritance—THE NATIONS! Your Word promises us that there will be a great shaking of nations. "Now He has promised, saying, 'Yet once more I will shake not only the earth but also the heavens'" (Hebrews 12:26).

We declare that this great shaking will help Christian believers overtake the Great Reset just as when God shook the walls of

Jericho down, enabling Joshua to overtake the Promised Land. We pray for the shaking of the Big Tech global monopoly that has become stronger than government to come down in the name of Jesus! We know the end from the beginning in God's Holy Word. We declare that Christ will rule over all nations of the earth.

> *For a child is born to us. A son is given to us; and the government will be on his shoulders. His name will be called Wonderful Counsellor, Mighty God, Everlasting Father, Prince of Peace. Of the increase of his government and of peace there shall be no end, on David's throne, and on his kingdom, to establish it, and to uphold it with justice and with righteousness from that time on, even forever. The zeal of the LORD of Armies will perform this (Isaiah 9:6-7).*

We agree with Daniel's prophecy that God (the ancient of days) will set up a worldwide kingdom replacing all existing nations for His son, Jesus, to rule as a worldwide permanent kingdom inheritance.

> *In the days of those kings the God of heaven will set up a kingdom which will never be destroyed, nor will its sovereignty be left to another people; but it will break in pieces and consume all these kingdoms, and it will stand forever (Daniel 2:44).*

> *I saw in the night visions, and behold, there came with the clouds of the sky one like a son of man, and he came even to the ancient of days, and they brought him near before him. Dominion was given him, and glory, and a kingdom, that all the peoples, nations, and languages should serve him. His do-*

minion is an everlasting dominion, which will not pass away, and his kingdom that which will not be destroyed (Daniel 7:13-14).

We agree with the Apostle Paul that Jesus Christ will become ruler over all the world!

Then the end comes, when he will deliver up the Kingdom to God, even the Father, when he will have abolished all rule and all authority and power. For he must reign until he has put all his enemies under his feet (1 Corinthians 15:24-25).

The seventh angel sounded, and great voices in heaven followed, saying, "The kingdom of the world has become the Kingdom of our Lord, and of his Christ. He will reign forever and ever!" (Revelation 11:15).

We thank You, Lord, that You told us in Your Word of these things that are to come and are happening now so that we would have courage to overcome.

"I have told you these things, so that in me you may have peace. In this world you will have trouble. But take heart! I have overcome the world" (John 16:33 NIV).

Amen!

THE PLEDGES
OF ALLEGIANCES

THE PLEDGE OF ALLEGIANCE
AMERICAN FLAG

Section 4 of the Flag Code states:
The Pledge of Allegiance to the Flag—"I pledge allegiance to the Flag of the United States of America, and to the Republic for which it stands, one Nation under God, indivisible, with liberty and justice for all"—should be rendered by standing at attention facing the flag with the right hand over the heart. When not in uniform, men should remove any nonreligious headdress with their right hand and hold it at the left shoulder, the hand being over the heart. Persons in uniform should remain silent, face the flag, and render the military salute."

THE PLEDGE OF ALLEGIANCE
CHRISTIAN FLAG

I pledge allegiance to the Christian Flag and to the Savior for whose Kingdom it stands. One Savior, crucified, risen, and coming again with life and liberty to all who believe. Amen.

THE PLEDGE OF ALLEGIANCE
BIBLE

I pledge allegiance to the Bible, God's Holy Word. I will make it a lamp unto my feet and a light unto my path and will hide its words in my heart that I might not sin against God. Amen.

THE PLEDGE OF ALLEGIANCE
APPEAL TO HEAVEN FLAG
BY DONICA PERRY HUDSON

I pledge allegiance to the Appeal to Heaven flag of Founding Father George Washington and to the everlasting God of Abraham, Isaac, and Jacob for which it stands, pledging as *a child of the Republic, to learn to live for my God, my land, and the union of the covenant United States of America.*

THE AMERICAN'S CREED
BY WILLIAM TYLER PAGE

I believe in the United States of America as a government of the people, by the people, for the people; whose just powers are derived from the consent of the governed, a democracy in a republic, a sovereign Nation of many sovereign States; a perfect union, one and inseparable; established upon those principles of freedom, equality, justice, and humanity for which American patriots sacrificed their lives and fortunes.

I therefore believe it is my duty to my country to love it, to support its Constitution, to obey its laws, to respect its flag, and to defend it against all enemies.

–Written 1917, accepted by the United States House of Representatives on April 3, 1918.

APPENDIX

From *The Naked Communist* by Cleon Skousen

CURRENT COMMUNIST GOALS

1. U.S. acceptance of coexistence as the only alternative to atomic war.
2. U.S. willingness to capitulate in preference to engaging in atomic war.
3. Develop the illusion that total disarmament [by] the United States would be a demonstration of moral strength.
4. Permit free trade between all nations regardless of Communist affiliation and regardless of whether or not items could be used for war.
5. Extension of long-term loans to Russia and Soviet satellites.
6. Provide American aid to all nations regardless of Communist domination.
7. Grant recognition of Red China. Admission of Red China to the U.N.

8. Set up East and West Germany as separate states in spite of Khrushchev's promise in 1955 to settle the German question by free elections under supervision of the U.N.

9. Prolong the conferences to ban atomic tests because the United States has agreed to suspend tests as long as negotiations are in progress.

10. Allow all Soviet satellites individual representation in the U.N.

11. Promote the U.N. as the only hope for mankind. If its charter is rewritten, demand that it be set up as a one-world government with its own independent armed forces. (Some Communist leaders believe the world can be taken over as easily by the U.N. as by Moscow. Sometimes these two centers compete with each other as they are now doing in the Congo.)

12. Resist any attempt to outlaw the Communist Party.

13. Do away with all loyalty oaths.

14. Continue giving Russia access to the U.S. Patent Office.

15. Capture one or both of the political parties in the United States.

16. Use technical decisions of the courts to weaken basic American institutions by claiming their activities violate civil rights.

17. Get control of the schools. Use them as transmission belts for socialism and current Communist propaganda. Soften the curriculum. Get control of teachers' associations. Put the party line in textbooks.

18. Gain control of all student newspapers.

19. Use student riots to foment public protests against programs or organizations which are under Communist attack.
20. Infiltrate the press. Get control of book-review assignments, editorial writing, policymaking positions.
21. Gain control of key positions in radio, TV, and motion pictures.
22. Continue discrediting American culture by degrading all forms of artistic expression. An American Communist cell was told to "eliminate all good sculpture from parks and buildings, substitute shapeless, awkward and meaningless forms."
23. Control art critics and directors of art museums. "Our plan is to promote ugliness, repulsive, meaningless art."
24. Eliminate all laws governing obscenity by calling them "censorship" and a violation of free speech and free press.
25. Break down cultural standards of morality by promoting pornography and obscenity in books, magazines, motion pictures, radio, and TV.
26. Present homosexuality, degeneracy and promiscuity as "normal, natural, healthy."
27. Infiltrate the churches and replace revealed religion with "social" religion. Discredit the Bible and emphasize the need for intellectual maturity which does not need a "religious crutch."
28. Eliminate prayer or any phase of religious expression in the schools on the ground that it violates the principle of "separation of church and state."

29. Discredit the American Constitution by calling it inadequate, old-fashioned, out of step with modern needs, a hindrance to cooperation between nations on a worldwide basis.
30. Discredit the American Founding Fathers. Present them as selfish aristocrats who had no concern for the "common man."
31. Belittle all forms of American culture and discourage the teaching of American history on the ground that it was only a minor part of the "big picture." Give more emphasis to Russian history since the Communists took over.
32. Support any socialist movement to give centralized control over any part of the culture--education, social agencies, welfare programs, mental health clinics, etc.
33. Eliminate all laws or procedures which interfere with the operation of the Communist apparatus.
34. Eliminate the House Committee on Un-American Activities.
35. Discredit and eventually dismantle the FBI.
36. Infiltrate and gain control of more unions.
37. Infiltrate and gain control of big business.
38. Transfer some of the powers of arrest from the police to social agencies. Treat all behavioral problems as psychiatric disorders which no one but psychiatrists can understand [or treat].
39. Dominate the psychiatric profession and use mental health laws as a means of gaining coercive control over those who oppose Communist goals.

40. Discredit the family as an institution. Encourage promiscuity and easy divorce.
41. Emphasize the need to raise children away from the negative influence of parents. Attribute prejudices, mental blocks and retarding of children to suppressive influence of parents.
42. Create the impression that violence and insurrection are legitimate aspects of the American tradition; that students and special-interest groups should rise up and use ["]united force["] to solve economic, political or social problems.
43. Overthrow all colonial governments before native populations are ready for self-government.
44. Internationalize the Panama Canal.
45. Repeal the Connally reservation so the United States cannot prevent the World Court from seizing jurisdiction [over domestic problems. Give the World Court jurisdiction] over nations and individuals alike.

SOURCE:
"Communist Goals (1963): Congressional Record – Appendix, pp. A34-A35," Tysknews.com, January 10, 1963, https://www.tysknews.com/Depts/New_World_Order/comgoals.htm.

ENDNOTES

INTRODUCTION

1. Wallnau, Lance, "Lance's Pentecost Webinar," Lance Wallnau Facebook Page Live Webinar, May 31, 2020, accessed August 20, 2020, https://www.facebook.com/watch/live/?v=253819582359027&ref=watch_permalink.

2. Jen Kirby, "Concentration camps and forced labor: China's repression of the Uighurs," explained, Vox.com, July 28, 2020, accessed August 20, 2020, https://www.vox.com/2020/7/28/21333345/uighurs-china-internment-camps-forced-labor-xinjiang.

3. 1600 Daily, "Why Americans lost faith in Washington," White-House.Gov, May 23, 2019, accessed August 21, 2020, https://twitter.com/whitehouse/status/1131919520237535232?lang=ca.

4. Mark Mekler, "Socialists Steam Millennials," Convention of States email report May 24, 2019, accessed August 2, 2019, https://us8.campaign-archive.com/?u=3a21cd3d06284c105dbd-92fee&id=1c3d6c5a63&e=ecbb767827.

5. Huckabee, Mike, "Generation Z goes adrift," MikeHuckabee. com, January 24, 2018, accessed February 22, 2019, https://www. mikehuckabee.com/latest-news?id=7a394b2d-d47a-491c-9810-d148fe93dbd9.

6. @Mr. Reagan, "The Brains Behind AOC Alexandria Ocasio-Cortez," YouTube.com, March 8, 2019, accessed August 12, 2020, https://www.youtube.com/watch?v=1h5iv6sECGU.

7. WokeHub.com author unnamed, "George Soros Funded Organizations Linked to Civil Unrest Across United States," May 30, 2020, accessed August 22, 2020, https://wokehub.com/u-s-news/george-soros-funded-organizations-linked-to-recent-civil-unrest-across-us/.

8. William J. Federer, *America's God and Country Encyclopedia of Quotations*, (St. Louis: Amerisearch Inc., 1994, 2013), 640.

9. Ibid, 641.

10. Ibid.

11. "The Prayer Life of George Washington," George Washington Inn & Estate, April 14, 2016, accessed May 17, 2020, https://www. georgewashingtoninn.com/the-prayer-life-of-george-washington.

12. The President of the United States of America, "Proclamation Appointing a National Fast Day," Abraham Lincoln Online, March 30, 1863, accessed July 31, 2020, http://www.abrahamlincolnonline.org/lincoln/speeches/fast.htm.

CHAPTER TWO

1. "Dr. Jeff Barkey questions the official COVID-19 narrative," New Manhattan Project, YouTube Video, 2:20, May 8,2020, accessed June 21, 2020, youtube.com/watch?v=HyKsG8KR0rY.

2. Ibid.

3. Ibid.

4. "Communist Goals (1963) Extension of Remarks of Hon. A.S. Herlong, Jr. of Florida in the House of Representatives," Congressional Record – Appendix, pp. A34-A35, Tysknews.com, January 10, 1963, accessed August 22, 2020, https://www.tysknews.com/Depts/New_World_Order/comgoals.htm.

5. Burkert, Henry, "10 Facts About Child Labor in China," BorgenProject.org, August 26, 2019, accessed July 31, 2020, https://borgenproject.org/10-facts-about-child-labor-in-china/.

6. Mike Maharrey, "A 'Living and Breathing' Constitution Is Really Dead", Tenth Amendment Center, Audio/Video, Maharrey Minute, June 10, 2020, accessed August 22, 2020, https://blog.tenthamendmentcenter.com/2020/06/a-living-and-breathing-constitution-is-really-dead/.

7. Tysknews.com, "Communist Goals (1963) Extension of Remarks of Hon. A.S. Herlong, Jr. of Florida in the House of Representatives," Congressional Record – Appendix, pp. A34-A35, January 10, 1963, accessed August 22, 2020, https://www.tysknews.com/Depts/New_World_Order/comgoals.htm.

8. "Rules for Radicals," Conservapedia, last modified June 16, 2020, last accessed August 22, 2020, https://www.conservapedia.com/Rules_for_Radicals.

9. Awr Hawkins, "How Saul Alinsky Taught Barack Obama Everything He Knows About Civic Upheaval," Breitbart.com, March 14, 2012, last accessed August 22, 2020, https://www.breitbart.com/politics/2012/03/14/how%20saul%20alinsky%20taught%20barack%20obama%20everything%20he%20knows%20about%20civic%20upheaval/.

10. Ibid.

11. "CNN Turns Blind Eye To Obama-Alinsky Ties," Investor's Business Daily, Editorials, January 26, 2012, last accessed August 22, 2020, https://www.investors.com/politics/editorials/media-ig-nores-obama-alinsky-rules-for-radicals/.

12. "Rules For Radicals," Conservapedia, last modified June 16, 2020, last accessed August 22, 2020, https://www.conservapedia.com/Rules_for_Radicals.

13. Alinsky, Saul, *Rules for Radicals*, (New York: Random House, 1971), Dedication.

14. Romans 10:9–10, 1 Timothy 2:5–6.

15. John 8:44, 2 Corinthians 5:17, 1 John 3:8.

16. Romans 6:23.

17. Romans 3:23.

18. Ephesians 2:8–9.

19. Stewart, Joe, "Again: Masterpiece Cakeshop sued for third time for refusing to make a cake that conflicted with owner's religious beliefs," Washington Insider, June 10, 2019, https://www.thewash-ingtoninsider.com/again-masterpiece-cakeshop-sued-for-third-time-for-refusing-to-make-a-cake-that-conflicted-with-owners-religious-beliefs/.

20. Ibid.

21. Jackson, Larry, interview by Donica Hudson, "Blessing Abortion Clinics," Truth Tellers Network, Video, February 19, 2019, https://donicahudson.com/videos/.

22. Decker, Cindy, interview by Donica Hudson, "Saving Charlotte, NC…What you can do," Truth Tellers Network, Video, June 8, 2020, https://donicahudson.com/videos/.

23. Hudson, Donica, "Christianity Today's Mark Galli thinks American Christians want all varieties of sexuality!," Truth Tellers Network, Video, 5:28, December 23, 2019, https://donicahudson.com/videos/.

CHAPTER THREE

1. Hudson, Donica, "BGEA Prayer September 28, 2017," Truth Tellers Network, Video, 17:04, September 28, 2017, https://donica-hudson.com/videos/.

2. Marini, John, *Politics by Other Means: The Use and Abuse of Scandal*, March 2019, https://imprimis.hillsdale.edu/politics-means-use-abuse-scandal/.

3. Ibid.

4. Ibid.

5. Ibid.

6. Ibid, 5.

7. Hudson, Donica, NC Conservatives, Video, 9:58, January 28, 2019, https://donicahudson.com/videos/.

8. Hayes, Christal, "Trump: Pulitzers awarded to NYT, Washington Post should be revoked for 'fake' Russia coverage," USATODAY.com, March 29, 2019, https://www.usatoday.com/story/news/politics/2019/03/29/president-trump-pulitzer-new-york-times-washington-post/3316086002/.

9. "Rules For Radicals," Conservapedia, last modified June 16, 2020, https://www.conservapedia.com/Rules_for_Radicals.

10. Genesis 12:3 (NIV).

11. Pierce, Chuck, "The Election…A New Era!," *Charisma*, November 14, 2012, https://www.charismamag.com/spirit/prophecy/15803-the-election-a-new-era?showall=1.

12. 1 Timothy 2:1–2 (NIV).

13. Matthew Staver Correspondent, email message to author, June 1, 2019.

14. Olasky, Marvin, *Prodigal Press*, (Phillipsburg, NJ: P&R Publishing Company, 2013).

15. Muesing, Alison, et.al., *His Kingdom Come*, (Seattle: YWAM Publishing, 2008), 391.

16. Wallnau, Lance, God's Chaos Candidate: Donald J. Trump and the American Unraveling, (Keller, TX: Killer Sheep Media, Inc., 2016), 50.

17. Ibid.

CHAPTER FOUR

1. 2 Corinthians 12:2–4.

2. Matthew 6:9–13 (NIV).

3. "Cultural Impact Team Manual," Introduction, Family Research Council, 2011, https://downloads.frc.org/EF/EF11C74.pdf

4. Ibid.

5. Ibid.

6. Proverbs 6:16–19.

7. Wallnau, Lance, Lance Wallnau, YouTube, https://www.youtube.com/user/LanceWallnauSr.

8. Pierce, Chuck, "The Death of the Early Church," *Apostolic Church Arising,* (Denton, Texas: Glory of Zion International Ministries, Inc., 2015), 45.

9. Ibid, 45–46.

10. Burke, Edmund (in a letter addressed to Thomas Mercer), Open Culture, "March 13, 2016, http://www.openculture.com/2016/03/edmund-burkeon-in-action.html.

11. Cahn, Jonathan, "The Elijah Paradigm," adapted from Gateway Church, March 11, 2017, https://gatewaypeople.com/sermons/the-elijah-paradigm.

CHAPTER FIVE

1. Exodus 32:12–14; 33:1; Leviticus 26:42; Deuteronomy 1:8; 4:31; 7:8; 9:27; 29:12–13; Joshua 21:44; 24:3–4; Psalms 105:8–10, 42–43; 2 Kings 13:23; 1 Chronicles 16:15–17; Micah 7:20; Nehemiah 9:7–8.

2. Booker, Richard, "The Miracle of the Scarlet Thread," (South Plainfield, NJ: Bridge Publishing, Inc., 1981), 26.

3. "The Scarlet Thread of Redemption," New King James Version of the Open Bible, (Nelson Publishing, 2019), 1365.

4. Galatians 4:4–6.

5. Booker, Richard, "The Miracle of the Scarlet Thread," (South Plainfield, NJ: Bridge Publishing, Inc., 1981), 27.

6. Ibid.

7. Ibid, 29.

8. Ibid, 30.

9. Ibid.

10. Ibid.

11. Ibid, 31.

12. Ibid.

13. Ibid.

14. Ibid, 37.

15. Crabtree, William Thomas, *Our Covenant-Constitution: The Covenantal Nature of the United States Constitution, Senior Thesis*, p. 5–6, Spring 2012, https://digitalcommons.liberty.edu/cgi/viewcontent.cgi?referer=https://www.bing.com/&httpsredir=1&article=1319&context=honors.

16. Ibid, 8.

17. Adler, Mortimer J., *Annals of America*, (Encyclopaedia Brittanica, 1968), 2:276.

18. Booker, Richard, "The Miracle of the Scarlet Thread," (South Plainfield, NJ: Bridge Publishing, Inc., 1981), 38.

19. Ibid, 41.

20. Crouch, Andrae, *The Blood Will Never Lose Its Power (Lyrics)*, YouTube Video, 4:15, March 12, 2017, https://www.youtube.com/watch?v=RUaPifIayjs.

CHAPTER SIX

1. Chavda, Bonnie, interview by Donica Hudson, "Bonnie Chavda: Mt Rushmore, the Heavenly Senate and Congress," Video, August 26, 2020, https://donicahudson.com/videos/

2. Liardon, Roberts, *We Saw Heaven*, (Shippenburg, PA: Destiny Image Publishers, Inc., 2000), 34.

3. Clement, Kim, "Kim Clement Trump Prophecies All Trump Prophecies, 9 11 & More! From 1996-2015," YouTube video, 16:53, December 20, 2019, https://www.youtube.com/watch?v=Fh-2hfbcPjOw.

4. Lamb, Joy, interview by Donica Hudson, "Donica Interviews Joy Lamb," Video, October 19, 2016, https://donicahudson.com/videos/

5. Lincoln, Abraham, "National Day of Prayer: Abraham Lincoln's Prayer for Our Nation," America World Adoption, May 6, 2015, https://awaa.org/blog/national-day-of-prayer-abraham-lincolns-prayer-for-our-nation/.

6. "Trump: 'In America we don't worship government, we worship God,'" YouTube Video, 5:11, July 2, 2017, https://www.bing.com/videos/search?q=Itrump+WE+DON%e2%80%99T+WORSHIP+GOVERNMENT+WE+WORSHIP+GOD&docid=608055811676835814&mid=3864B004243AA294AD3F-3864B004243AA294AD3F&view=detail&FORM=VIRE.

CHAPTER SEVEN

1. Clarke, Adam, *The New Testament of Our Lord and Savior Jesus Christ, Commentary and Critical Notes of the Sacred Writings*, (London: 1817), 1:5, https://books.google.com/books?id=I6k-GAAAAQAAJ&pg=RA1-PT494#v=onepage&q=adam%20clarke%20angels%20ascending%20and%20descending%20metaphor&f=false.

2. The Mecklenburg Declaration–Declaration Text, (number 3), Mecklenburg Historical Association, (Raleigh: Published by the Governor, 1831) 13–14, https://www.meckdec.org/declaration/the-text.

3. Glasgow, W.M., "The Editors Introduction," June 1, 1895, TrueCovenanter.com, "Renewal of the Covenants, National and Solemn League; A Confession of Sins and Engagement to Duties by Alexander Craighead," November 11, 1743.

4. "Benjamin Franklin and the Presbyterians," Log College Press Blog, February 19, 2018, https://www.logcollegepress.com/blog/2018/2/14/benjamin-franklin-and-the-presbyterians?rq=benjamin%20franklin%20and%20the%20presbyterians.

5. Matthew 12:45.

6. Sparks, Larry, *Prophetic Words for 2020*, (Shippensburg, PA: Destiny Image Publishers, Inc. 2020), 135.

7. Blackaby, Henry, interview by Donica Hudson, "Henry Blackaby on Charlotte Alive," Truth Tellers Network, Video, September 1, 2016, https://donicahudson.com/videos/

8. Barillas, Martin M., "Ben Shapiro: This time, leftist radicals are coming for Catholics first, then us Jews," LifeSite News, February 20, 2019, https://www.lifesitenews.com/news/ben-shapiro-this-time-leftist-radicals-are-coming-for-catholics-first.

9. Ibid.

10. Stepman, Jarrett, "The Fathers of Communism Were Racist," The Daily Signal, July 13, 2020, https://www.dailysignal.com/2020/07/13/the-fathers-of-communism-were-racist/.

11. Ibid.

12. Crabtree, William Thomas, *Our Covenant-Constitution: The Covenantal Nature of the United States Constitution, Senior Thesis*, p. 22, Spring 2012, https://digitalcommons.liberty.edu/cgi/viewcontent.cgi?referer=https://www.bing.com/&httpsredir=1&article=1319&context=honors.

13. "Washington's Changing Views on Slavery" George Washington's Mount Vernon, https://www.mountvernon.org/george-washington/slavery/washingtons-changing-views-on-slavery/.

14. Ibid.

15. Ibid.

16. Ibid.

17. "Civil War Biography Abraham Lincoln" Battlefields. org, https://www.battlefields.org/learn/biographies/abraham-lincoln.

18. Abraham Lincoln Online - Speeches and Writings, *Proclamation Appointing a National Fast Day*, March 30, 1863, http://www.abrahamlincolnonline.org/lincoln/speeches/fast.htm.

19. Hudson, Donica, "An Invitation of Honor," Truth Tellers Network, Video, 5:33, September 1, 2016, https://donicahudson.com/videos/.

20. Vaynol, Andre, interview by Donica Hudson, "Breaking the North Carolina Drought Pastor Andre Vaynol," Truth Tellers Network, Video, August 31, 2016, https://donicahudson.com/videos/.

21. Bigpond, Negiel, interview by Donica Hudson, "Removing the Curse from the Land," Truth Tellers Network, Video, September 5, 2016, https://donicahudson.com/videos/.

22. Pastor Andre Vaynol, Negiel Bigpond, Ellen Day Purim, interviews by Donica Hudson, "Native American Reconciliation Series," Truth Tellers Network, Videos, https://donicahudson.com/videos/.

23. Jim Daly, interview by Donica Hudson, "Donica interviews Jim Daly, Pres. FOCUS ON THE FAMILY," Truth Tellers Network, Video, July 12, 2019, https://donicahudson.com/videos/.

24. Sheets, Dutch, "Dutch Sheets 2020 [STRONG MESSAGE] Activating The Power Of God (Must Watch)," Prophecy Center, YouTube Video, 1:21:56, July 23, 2020, https://www.youtube.com/watch?v=eRlWju_Bhr8.

25. Ibid.

26. Bridges, Dr. Kynan, My SHOCKING Dream About President Donald J. Trump (You must watch), Dr. Kynan Bridges, Facebook Live Video, 14:20, July 10, 2020, https://www.facebook.com/PastorKynanBridges/videos/404799440480071.

27. Ibid.

28. Ibid.

29. Ibid.

30. Ibid.

31. Federer, William J., *America's God and Country Encyclopedia of Quotations*, (Fame Publishing, Inc., 1859), 636.

32. Ibid, 637.

CHAPTER EIGHT

1. Isaiah 54:5, 61:10, 62:5, Hosea 2:19–20.

2. Romans 7:4; 2 Corinthians 11:2; Ephesians 5:23; Revelation 19:7–9, 21:2–4, 9.

3. Adams, John, "From John Adams Massachusetts Militia," Founders.archives.gov, October 11, 1798 https://founders.archives.gov/documents/Adams/99-02-02-3102.

4. Stepman, Jarrett, "The Fathers of Communism Were Racist," The Daily Signal, July 13, 2020, https://www.dailysignal.com/2020/07/13/the-fathers-of-communism-were-racist/.

5. "Oath of Office (Officer)," PACE Profession of Arms Center of Excellence, https://www.airman.af.mil/Portals/17/002%20 All%20Products/006%20Trifolds/Oath_Pamphlet_for_Officer. pdf?ver=2015-12-22-113949-437.

6. Ibid.

7. Stepman, Jarrett, "The Fathers of Communism Were Racist," The Daily Signal, July 13, 2020, https://www.dailysignal. com/2020/07/13/the-fathers-of-communism-were-racist/.

8. Johnson, Darryl. 2020. "As I was walking this morning seeking the Lord, the Holy Spirit said this to me," Facebook, August 10, 2020, 9:51 A.M., https://www.facebook.com/darryl.johnson.129.

9. Ibid.

10. Jefferson, Thomas, "United States Declaration of Independence," July 4, 1776.

11. Lincoln, Abraham, "A Prayer for Our Nation," Washington DC.

12. Hostetler, Bob, "Six Ways to Pray Like Abraham Lincoln" Guideposts, February 12, 2016, https://www.guideposts.org/ faith-and-prayer/prayer-stories/pray-effectively/6-ways-to-pray-like-abraham-lincoln.

13. Washington, George, 1919, Printed Ephemera: Three Centuries of Broadsides and Other Printed Ephemera (10,182).

14. Johnson, William J., *George Washington, The Christian*, (New York: The Abingdon Press, 1919).

15. Federer, William J., *America's God and Country Encyclopedia of Quotations*, (Amerisearch, Inc. 1994), 636.

16. Ibid, 637.

17. Ibid, 639.

18. Ibid, 645.

19. Ibid, 645–646.

20. Ibid, 639.

21. Ibid, p.636

22. Ibid, p. 637

23. Ibid, p. 659

24. Ibid, p. 645

25. Ibid, p. 660

26. Jefferson, Thomas, "Thomas Jefferson on God, Scripture, and Prayer," Family Council, May 28, 2015, https://familycouncil.org/?p=12148.

27. Stephen McDowell and Mark Beliles, *The American Dream: Jamestown and the Planting of the American Christian Republic*, (Providence Foundation, April 2, 2007).

28. "First Amendment," History.com, updated September 25, 2019, https://www.history.com/topics/united-states-constitution/first-amendment.

29. Allum Bokhari, "Who Is in Control? The Need to Rein in Big Tech," *Imprimis* 50, no. 1 (January 2021): 4, Who Is in Control? The Need to Rein in Big Tech - Imprimis (hillsdale.edu)

30. "Absolute Proof—Exposing Election Fraud and the Theft of America by Enemies Foreign and Domestic," Evidence that elections are being stolen worldwide—by Mike Lindell, StopWorldControl.com, https://www.stopworldcontrol.com/mike/; Dinesh Souza, "2000 Mules," Dinesh.locals, May 07, 2022, accessed May 07, 2022, https://dinesh.locals.com/upost/2083099/2000-mules.

31. Virginia Foxx ,"Foxx Report," March 4, 2022 (email newsletter)

ENDNOTES

32. "The Great Reset Explained in 5 Minutes," January 9, 2021, https://www.youtube.com/watch?v=f9MfjkBCUH0

33. "World Economic Forum Presents: The Great Reset—"You'll own nothing and you'll be happy," Nov. 14, 2020, https://www.youtube.com/watch?v=4zUjsEaKbkM

34. "The Great Reset Explained in 5 Minutes," January 9, 2021, https://www.youtube.com/watch?v=f9MfjkBCUH0

35. Bill Gates, "Innovating to zero!" TED video, 27:33. February 26, 2010, https://www.ted.com/talks/bill_gates_innovating_to_zero/transcript?language=en#t-304738, 04:27–04:48 min.

36. James Corbett, "Bill Gates And Population Control," HoweStreet.com, May 16, 2020, https://www.howestreet.com/2020/05/bill-gates-and-population-control/.

37. Alex Newman, "The Great Reset," *New American* magazine, January 4, 2021, p. 3.

38. Ibid, p. 3.

39. James Corbett, "Bill Gates And Population Control," HoweStreet.com, May 16, 2020, https://www.howestreet.com/2020/05/bill-gates-and-population-control/.

40. "Yuval Noah Harari: The 2021 60 Minutes interview," Oct. 31, 2021, https://www.youtube.com/watch?v=EIVTf-C6oQo, 07:05-07:12.

41. "World Economic Forum Presents: The Great Reset—"You'll own nothing and you'll be happy," Nov. 14, 2020, https://www.youtube.com/watch?v=4zUjsEaKbkM

42. Michael Rectenwald, "What Is the Great Reset?" *Imprimis* publication, December 2021, Vol. 50 No. 12, p. 3.

43. Ibid, p. 3.

44. Ibid, p. 3.

45. "Yuval Noah Harari | 21 Lessons for the 21st Century | Talks at Google" video, Oct. 11, 2018, https://www.youtube.com/watch?v=Bw9P_ZXWDJU, 10:33-10:46 minutes.

46. "Yuval Noah Harari: Humans are now hackable animals" video, CNN Connect The World, https://www.cnn.com/videos/world/2019/11/26/yuval-noah-harari-interview-anderson-vpx.cnn, 01:36-5:10

47. "This is the End" video by Greg Reese, Banned.Video, July 14, 2021, https://banned.video/watch?id=60ef095dc63e855fe-6a48b8f.

48. Ibid.

49. "Biden Stakes Claim to Lead New World Order, Warns of Russian Cyberattack" by Mark Pellin, *Headline USA*, March 22, 2022, https://headlineusa.com/biden-stakes-claim-to-lead-new-world-order-warns-of-russian-cyberattack/.

50. "The West's response to Russia & Ukraine FINALLY makes sense," The Glenn Beck Program, March 2, 2022, https://www.youtube.com/watch?v=HlBXTeeM710.

51. Warren Mass, "At World Economic Forum in Davos, Biden Urges Defense of 'Liberal International Order'", *New American*, January 18, 2017, https://thenewamerican.com/at-world-economic-forum-in-davos-biden-urges-defense-of-liberal-international-order/.

52. Yuval Noah Harari: Humans are now hackable animals" video, CNN Connect The World, https://www.cnn.com/videos/world/2019/11/26/yuval-noah-harari-interview-anderson-vpx.cnn, 11:31-11:41 minutes.

53. "Yuval Noah Harari | 21 Lessons for the 21st Century | Talks at Google" video, Oct. 11, 2018, https://www.youtube.com/watch?v=Bw9P_ZXWDJU, 27:28-27:33 minutes

54. Ibid, 18:24-18:26 minutes.

55. "WEF Top Advisor: Covid is Critical to Total Biometric Surveillance," OneNewsPage.com, April 8, 2022, https://www.onenewspage.com/video/20220401/14606402/WEF-Top-Advisor-Covid-is-Critical-to-Total.htm, 01:14-01:28.

56. BlueletterBible.org, Strong's Concordance G5331, https://www.blueletterbible.org/lexicon/g5331/kjv/tr/0-1/

57. Dr. Michael McDowell, "In Response To The Vaccine" Part 1 video, Bitchute.com, https://www.bitchute.com/video/94OEMQT31gp2/, August 14, 2021.

58. "About My Bindle." Bindle, April 26, 2021. Joinbindle.com/learnmore/.

59. "Pfizer Hid This Shocking Data," Liberty Counsel Action, April 8, 2022, https://lcaction.org/detail/220408-pfizer-hid-this-shocking-data.

60. Janis Siegel, "Nanotechnology Used in Covid Vaccines, 2,000 Foods, Goes Unlabeled," The Epoch Times, March 4, 2022, https://www.theepochtimes.com/nanoparticles-being-used-in-more-food-and-drugs_4303477.html?utm_source=Morningbrief&utm_campaign=mb-2022-04-10&utm_medium=email&est=dJtXMVZqKUb-b%2Bh%2FQ9Cop4aQi0kFE1I3lDD6htyLGBgH5O4QK7v-VeSNv%2F6Y26ue8Yu877.

61. "Dr. Carrie Medej: COVID Shots Facilitate Transhumanism" by Randolph Jason, Gospel News Network, July 6, 2021, https://gospelnewsnetwork.org/2021/07/06/dr-carrie-madej-covid-shots-facilitate-transhumanism/.

62. Janis Siegel, "Nanotechnology Used in Covid Vaccines, 2,000 Foods, Goes Unlabeled," The Epoch Times, March 4, 2022, https://www.theepochtimes.com/nanoparticles-being-used-in-more-food-and-drugs_4303477.html?utm_source=Morningbrief&utm_campaign=mb-2022-04-10&utm_medium=email&est=dJtXMVZqKUb-b%2Bh%2FQ9Cop4aQi0kFE1I3lDD6htyLGBgH5O4QK7v-VeSNv%2F6Y26ue8Yu877.

63. "Panel Discussion: Technology and the Future of Democracy," Athens Democracy Forum, Oct. 3, 2020, https://www.youtube.com/watch?v=W2z2dufityI, 31:55-33:02 minutes.

64. Allum Bokhari, "Who Is In Control? The Need to Rein in Big Tech," Imprimis, January 2021, Volume 50, No. 1

65. Carlo Maria Viganò, Tit. Archbishop of Ulpiana, "Open Letter to the President of the United States Donald J. Trump, October 25, 2020.

66. Executive Order No. 83 by Governor Bill Lee, State of Tennessee, August 6, 2021, Paragraph 8, p. 5.

67. Mike Adams, "Red Alert: Covid internment camps announced in America; Tennessee governor signs EO authorizing National Guard to carry out medical kidnappings," Natural News, August 10, 2021, https://www.naturalnews.com/2021-08-10-covid-internment-camps-announced-in-america-tennessee-cdc-internment.html

68. Patrick Howley, "Exclusive: National Guard Posts, Deletes, Reposts 13 Internment/Resettlement Specialist Job Listings Mostly Near Jails and Prisons, Stunning DoD Directive states that 'civilian internees' may lawfully be detained," National File, August 26, 2021, https://nationalfile.com/exclusive-national-guard-posts-deletes-re-posts-13-internment-resettlement-specialist-job-listings-mostly-near-jails-and-prisons/

69. Raymond Wolfe, "CDC Discussed Strategy to Isolate People Inside Refugee Camps to Stop COVID-19," Lifesite News, August 17, 2021, https://www.lifesitenews.com/news/cdc-discussed-strategy-to-isolate-people-inside-refugee-camps-to-stop-covid-19/

70. Ibid.

71. Alex Newman, "The Great Reset-Deep State globalists taking over the world and you!," *New American* magazine, January 4, 2021, p. 1

72. Ibid, p. 2

73. "W02020060606 – Cryptocurrency System Using Body Activity Data," PatentScope, World Intellectual Property Organization (WIPO), Patent published 3-26-2020 to Microsoft, https://patentscope.wipo.int/search/en/detail.jsf?docId=WO2020060606&tab=PCTDESCRIPTION.

74. "Bill Gates will use microchip implants to fight coronavirus," Biohackinfo News, 3-19-2020, https://biohackinfo.com/news-bill-gates-id2020-vaccine-implant-covid-19-digital-certificates/.

75. "Bill Gates Vaccine Ingredient Says it All : An Enzyme Called LUCIFERASE is What Makes Bill Gates Implantable Vaccine Work — VACCINE ID," Stillness In The Storm, September 4, 2020, https://stillnessinthestorm.com/2020/09/must-read-an-enzyme-called-luciferase-is-what-makes-bill-gates-implantable-vaccine-work-vaccine-id/.

76. "Nano coronavirus recombinant vaccine taking graphene oxide as carrier," Patent pending CN112220919A, China Publication 1-15-2021, https://patents.google.com/patent/CN112220919A/en.

77. "DARPA Hydrogel in COVID Vaccine can create crystals, nano-antennas to receive signals from 5G Tower," Space Traveler in Alabama, May 19, 2021, https://spacetravelinalabama. com/2021/05/19/darpa-hydrogel-in-covid-vaccine-can-create-crystals-nano-antennas-to-receive-signals-from-5g-tower/.

78. Bill Gates, "Innovating to zero!" TED video, 27:33. February 26, 2010, https://www.ted.com/talks/bill_gates_innovating_to_ zero/transcript?language=en#t-304738, 04:27–04:48 min.

79. Alex Newman, "The Great Reset-Deep State globalists taking over the world and you!," The New American magazine, January 4, 2021, p. 4.

80. Ibid.

81. William Federer, "Understanding the Culture with William Federer," YouTube video, 1:08:13, posted by "Real Life with Jack Hibbs," August 11, 2021, https://www.youtube.com/ watch?v=aOysMK5xK5c.

82. Dr. Christiane Northrup, "An Evil Agenda by Bloodline Families," Bitchute video, 38:34, posted by "SGT REPORT," August 18, 2021, https://www.bitchute.com/video/ZutSRWBp6v0c/.

83. Steve Barwick, "Occult Ritual Transformation and Coronavirus: How Mask Wearing, Hand Washing, 'Social Separation' and Lockdowns Are Age-Old Occult Rituals Being Used to Initiate People Into a New Global Order," Have Ye Not Read?, May 19, 2020, https://haveyenotread.com/occult-ritual-transformation-and-coronavirus/?fbclid=IwAR0N8ou4abDVS-BuDg56G5mxMI7sD8ew-pG23jz5zUgzhfsVsVJ6rnGa5Mbw.

84. Ibid.

85. Alex Newman, "The Great Reset-Deep State globalists taking over the world and you!," The New American magazine, January 4, 2021, p. 8.

86. Ibid, p. 2.

ABOUT THE AUTHOR

DONICA GRADUATED from Wake Forest University with a B.A. in English, minor emphasis in Radio/TV/Film and as the university's #1 Female Tournament Karate Fighter. She completed post-graduate ministerial studies at Jubilee International Training Center in San Jose, California. She is an ordained pastor, certified in global trauma healing at SIM's Trauma Healing Institute and is the nonprofit founder of IHP Global Ministries, Inc.

Donica has effectively executed and participated in numerous local and national prayer events and activism events to protect religious liberty. As a revivalist, she created and hosted *Charlotte Alive*, a TV show on revival and spiritual awakening airing in Charlotte, North Carolina and South Africa. As a faith activist, Donica drafted a "Proclamation For A Day of Prayer, Fasting, and Humility for North Carolina" signed by former North Carolina Governor Pat McCrory, which became the focal prayer point during the Charlotte Riots at a Clergy Press Conference. Donica issued a national "Invitation of Honor" by video and personal mail to America's fifty

Governors, encouraging them to proclaim Days of Prayer, Fasting, and Humility to bring protection to their states.

Donica cofounded North Carolinians For Privacy, a group launched to protect the privacy of girls and women in public bathrooms, showers, and locker rooms when she and her husband sued the Federal Government over this issue. Donica also campaigned for President Trump on the Congressional Wives Speakers Bus Tour in 2016, participating at Clergy Roundtables with Donald Trump and Eric and Lara Trump.

Having hosted over 120 television shows since 2004, Donica Hudson became known as the "go-to media personality" for Charlotte's faith-based community.

Also respected in Charlotte's sports and business world, Donica served as chaplain for the CHARLOTTE STING (WNBA Team), Vice President of the CHARLOTTE CHRISTIAN CHAMBER OF COMMERCE (C3), and a prayer leader for Charlotte Awake, spearheading prayer efforts at the Billy Graham Library. Currently, Donica serves on the Charlotte Coalition (Leaders uniting for Religious Liberty) and the Legislative Prayer Caucus.

Donica will tell you that her greatest accomplishment is her strong marriage with husband, Todd, and their three beautiful children, Davis, Salem, and Lucas. The Hudsons reside in the North Carolina mountains.

Made in USA - North Chelmsford, MA
13744_9781633374300
10.05.2023 1349